Good Books books may be purchased in bulk at special discounts for sales promotion, corporate gifts, fund-raising, or educational purposes. Special editions can also be created to specifications. For details, contact the Special Sales Department, Good Books, 307 West 36th Street, 11th Floor, New York, NY 10018 or info@skyhorsepublishing.com.

Good Books is an imprint of Skyhorse Publishing, Inc.®, a Delaware corporation.

Visit our website at www.goodbooks.com.

10 9 8 7 6 5 4 3 2

Library of Congress Cataloging-in-Publication Data is available on file.

Cover design by Laura Klynstra
Cover photograph by Emily Hutchinson

Special thanks for:
Editing: Nicole Frail
Christmas sign: Kala Klein designs
Flowers: Sprig Flower Co.
New cake stands: Amalfi Decor
Cookie cutters: Posh Little Designs, Baked on Brighton
Vintage items from the kitchen and from the drawer: Celia Johnson
Barn for Christmas shoot: The Younger Family

Print ISBN: 978-1-68099-484-1
Ebook ISBN: 978-1-68099-485-8

Printed in China

To Mike and the Kids—

This book is a piece of our story together, so thank you for helping me make it possible. You make me better every day of my life. Baking and decorating gives me joy because of the excitement you have shown me from the beginning. I am inspired by you in all that I do. We have been through so much as a family and are stronger today than ever before. We know all too well how short life is, and I know that's why we hold each other so close. I cherish the memories we have made over the years in the kitchen together. I know there are more fun days of baking and decorating ahead. This book is for you. We are, forever, all in!

Contents

Introduction

How It All Started

Let's go back to the "before the beginning," so I can help you see the big picture of how it started.

When I was a little girl, I loved nothing more than being in the kitchen and baking with my Grandma Loopie (yes, Loopie means crazy, but in the most perfect way). I was always in awe of her as I watched her bake. I caught on very fast and loved cracking eggs, measuring flour, and sampling the goodies. She taught me the basics of baking and shared some secret recipes with me that my family still treasures. My grandmother was such a patient teacher while having the sweetest way of making me feel like I could do anything. Sadly, my family and I lost her to cancer, and baking didn't feel the same after she was gone. The passion was still in my heart, but I just pushed it aside.

Beauty from Ashes

Fast forward to having two amazing children, Reese and Nick, to meeting my husband Mike, who became their stepdad. Mike and I decided to have a child of our own in 2007 and named her Jennifer Louise after my mother and grandmother. We loved on her so much; she was the piece that solidified our family. When Jenny was two and a half months old, she suddenly passed away in her sleep; it was classified as SIDS because they couldn't find a reason for her death. This left us broken, angry, and beyond devastated. We were all hurting so much from losing her. How could we go on living life without our child?

Time seemed to go on, but I was stuck. We decided to get pregnant right away in the midst of our grief. We were blessed when our son Mikie came along in 2009. He was born exactly one year and 10 days after Jenny had passed. Having him felt like our family was once again complete. Everyone told us how strong we were, but little did everyone know, Mike and I were still in so much pain from losing Jenny.

With all these wonderful things happening, I still had this ache in my heart. This hole that still left me half alive. Reese, Nick, and Mikie brought every joy and light into my life. My children were the reason I got up every day, but I was still struggling. It's hard to explain that loss unless you have lived it. Losing a child feels like your heart is physically broken. We were all trying to survive this together.

A few years after Mikie was born, friends of ours invited us to the Grove Church in Marysville. Something happened that day to my husband and me. God lifted us up, opened our eyes, and met us right where we were. We began finding joy in the everyday things. My family and I started attending regularly. The Grove does a community outreach every summer where they volunteer to clean up parks, paint and clean schools, and serve for a week out of the summer. That hooked us because we could now see a purpose and a bigger picture of what God

was doing. We shifted our eyes toward Jesus and away from everything else. For the first time since we lost our Jenny, we found hope.

With that newfound hope came the desire to really live my life fully for my family so I decided to start baking again. I realized how much I had missed it. Somehow being in the kitchen baking and creating was helping me find myself. I can look at a blank cookie and see so many possibilities. My mom and my sisters will joke with me about not being able to draw a stick figure to save my life, but as soon as I pick up a piping bag, magic happens.

In using these special techniques, I have set

myself apart. I'm a self-taught baker with a background from Grandma Loopie, Betty Crocker, and old-school Wilton decorating books. I also created videos to show people how to frost cookies with buttercream frosting. I would look around and see beautiful bouquets of flowers and think, *how can I make this a cookie?* My passion had now turned into a business: The Hutch Oven.

Baking and decorating has always been a safe haven for me. It has been a stress relief; I am in a peaceful place as I decorate beautiful cookies. The best way to describe my mission with The Hutch Oven is that I want to keep my daughter's memory alive as I share my story of hope. I thought a book would be the perfect place to not only share what I'm deeply passionate about but encourage whoever may read this that you can do it, too! The step-by-step photos allow anyone to learn these techniques.

Let's Get Familiar

The techniques I'm sharing with you work best for me, so with that being said, if you have a way that works better, then please use it. My hope is that I can prevent you from the fails and disasters I've had along the way, from powdered sugar explosions and wilted-looking petals, to overbaked cookies that had to be thrown out. My recipes have evolved over the years, as has my baking. I think the way for us to learn and grow is from failures and mistakes.

I use circles, squares, and rectangles in many different ways. I do love a cute cookie cutter, but I realize that not everyone has them. You can find templates online to print out and trace cookie shapes with a knife. I find a lot of inexpensive cookie cutters at secondhand stores and online.

Presentation is key; beautiful cookies deserve a beautiful plate. I have searched and scoured eBay, antique stores, and the Internet for the most beautiful cake plates and serving trays. I also love a beautiful modern cake plate; these are timeless. You will see my style throughout the book, and I hope it inspires you to pick up some cake plates too.

know how to execute. I'm here to help with all of that.

I will share master tips along the way. These have been especially helpful to me!

Keep Going

I am a firm believer that women are supposed to encourage each other. I almost quit baking years ago because I was antagonized by another baker, but I knew that my purpose was bigger, so I trusted in God's plan and kept going. Maybe you are struggling with something, maybe you are looking for direction, fulfillment, or just a new joy in your life. I'm here to tell you that you deserve it. Go after it, and don't let anyone try to stop you. Make sure to lift people up on the way to your success, because someday you'll want to turn around and see all the people cheering you on, not look back to see people you have stepped on to get to where you are. Always support and lift up.

It helps if you read through the recipe and instructions in its entirety before you even start baking. I like to make sure I'm prepped and ready, so I can bake and frost without having to run to the store. It helps to plan what you need in advance. If you pick out a plate of cookies you want to decorate, write down everything you need so you're ready to go. Throughout the book, I have used the same tips numerous times in decorating different plates of cookies to make it easier. I also want you to get familiar with new tips and techniques you may not have seen before, or maybe you have seen but don't

Baking and decorating should be fun, should bring you joy and happiness. You are baking and creating delicious masterpieces for your friends and family. Maybe it's for a potluck, bake sale, church auction, child's birthday, baby shower, or you want to start a business. No matter the occasion, there's always a reason to bake someone happy.

So come on, friends, let's start baking memories and have some fun!

Psalm 34:8 *Taste and see that the LORD is good, blessed is the one who takes refuge in him.*

How to Use this Book

I have outlined the book so you have things you need **From the kitchen** and **From the drawer.**

From the kitchen are the cookies and buttercream you will need. I also have things listed like mashed berries, lemon juice, hot water, or things you would make or get from the kitchen. *From the drawer* are things like tips, piping bags, spatulas, food colorings, sprinkles, and all the goodies needed to decorate that we generally keep in a drawer.

I recommend that you read the full instructions, techniques, ingredients, and master tips before you start on a cookie plate. Some of the master tips are very important to successful decorating and you don't want to miss that.

I try to clean as I go, but there are days that it looks like an explosion in my kitchen. Don't be too hard on yourself, and have fun!

If you can avoid it, do not substitute— use what is recommended in each recipe. I use Costco Salted Sweet Cream Butter and Crisco vegetable shortening in my signature recipes. There are some bakers that will turn their nose up at the shortening in buttercream. If you don't like that, all butter works great. The shortening gives the buttercream some extra smoothness for

piping my designs. If there isn't a Costco near you, Safeway's Lucerne Sweet Cream Butter will work. Otherwise, you can use unsalted butter and add ¼ teaspoon of salt when you are creaming the butter and shortening.

I always check the expiration dates, even on flour. Baking powder expires; check it.

Use the best ingredients. Vanilla extract needs to be pure. I know it's expensive, but it's a must.

Measuring ingredients for baking is a science and some may find it odd that I don't weigh my ingredients. My hope is that anyone can learn to make my cookies, whether you are a novice or an expert baker.

For my recipes, I use the scoop and level method. I use a spoon to scoop in flour or powdered sugar into my cup. The flour should mound over your cup. I do this over a plate or over the bag so there isn't a huge mess. Take the flat back of a butter knife or metal spatula and level off the measuring cup. When I pack my brown sugar, I scoop it in, pack it down with my hands, and make sure it's level before adding it.

I am not an expert in gluten-free or dairy-free baking, but I have added a couple recipes that are sensitive to those allergies. I want

these creative cookies to be enjoyed and loved by all. I have worked very hard to make them just right. I found that Earth Balance Soy-Free Buttery Spread in the tub works best for dairy-free. It doesn't have a strange taste like the Earth Balance sticks do. I use Bob's Red Mill 1 to 1 flour in my gluten-free cookie recipe.

Everyone has a different oven so please know your oven before you start baking. The cook time for the cookies is crucial. Bake them until they puff up or the time noted.

Keep your tips and decorating supplies organized; it's the worst when something is missing. I use a plastic organizer from the craft store to keep my tips and couplers. Always properly clean your tips, couplers, and cookie cutters after using and put them back in their place for the next time.

Essentials

Stand mixer:

A large mixer with a bowl that locks into place as it's mixing. They have many attachments; I use the paddle attachment throughout this book. It can operate on its own with a variation of speeds for mixing. Medium is my safe speed.

Offset or angled spatula:

Flat and thin with a handle used for spreading and smoothing. It is angled to keep your fingers off the icing. I use the 4-inch or 6-inch spatula. They also have tapered edges, which come in handy for the smaller designs.

Plastic coupler:

This is a plastic part that connects your tip to your piping bag and allows tips to be changed easily.

Piping or pastry bag:

Handheld bag made from cloth or plastic that holds the buttercream while decorating. I prefer the plastic bags.

Tips:

Small metal or plastic nozzles attached to the end of the piping bag that are an essential part of decorating. The sizes vary. The large tips do not require couplers. I prefer Wilton tips

Cookie cutters:

A sharp metal or plastic device made for cutting dough into all different shapes and sizes.

Mixing bowls:

A deep bowl that can mix ingredients together or, in this case, mix buttercream colors and flavors in small batches.

Wire cooling rack:

This will allow air to circulate through cookies to help the cooling process. Use a tight grid cooling rack for cookies.

Cookie sheet:

Even-heating rust-proof aluminum baking sheet or a nonstick baking sheet suitable for cookies.

Cookie spatula:

A flat, thin stainless-steel tool used to lift cookies off a baking sheet.

Rubber spatula:

An essential kitchen tool for gently scraping or stirring mixtures.

Wire whisk:

Used to blend ingredients.

Sifter:

Used to break up or separate clumps in the dry ingredients. You can also use a wire mesh strainer to sift.

Measuring cups and spoons:

Cups and spoons marked with amounts used for baking.

Techniques

FILLING YOUR PIPING BAG

From the kitchen
Batch of buttercream

From the drawer
Piping bags
Coupler
Tip
Scissors
Clear plastic wrap optional
(see Two-Toned
Buttercream instructions,
page 4)

Instructions

1. Cut your piping bag about 1 inch up from the tip.
2. Drop down your coupler.
3. Fill your bag halfway with buttercream (use about 1 cup).
4. Attach piping tip.

MASTER TIP

Don't overfill your buttercream. It warms up quickly in your hand and the flowers can get droopy. It's easier to pipe and guide your hand with less in your bag. Keep refilling for the best results.

SMOOTH BUTTERCREAM TECHNIQUE

From the kitchen
Batch of buttercream
Cookies
1 cup hot water

From the drawer
Angled spatula
Tip 5, 10, or 12
Kitchen towel

Instructions

1. Pipe on buttercream with tip 12 to cover cookie.

2. Smooth buttercream on your cookie with angled spatula.

3. Dip angled spatula in hot water for 10 seconds and quickly dry.

4. Smooth buttercream with heated spatula until smooth. Repeat if needed.

MASTER TIP

Continue to heat up the water and spatula and smooth the cookie until desired smoothness is achieved. Pipe different colors on the buttercream with a small round tip as you're smoothing to get a marbled look on the buttercream.

TWO-TONED BUTTERCREAM

I love this two-toned buttercream for my flowers. I will refer to these instructions throughout the book. This technique turns the petal tips colors. This keeps the buttercream in place, so it doesn't change how much color comes out halfway through piping. I use the plastic wrap trick even when I'm not using two colors because it makes it so easy to just grab out the plastic and throw it away. This method keeps the buttercream from warming up in your hand so quickly.

From the kitchen	From the drawer
Batch of buttercream	Clear plastic wrap
	Piping bag
	Coupler
	Tip
	Red gel food coloring

Instructions

1. Lay out a piece of plastic wrap long ways, or horizontally, and add a strip of red buttercream (or desired color).
2. Layer on white buttercream and cover the red.
3. Fold over hot-dog-style to create a pouch. Twist up your ends and coil up one side so the buttercream doesn't come out. With the other end, feed it though your coupler.
4. Cut the end of your piping bag about 1 inch and drop in the end with attached coupler.
5. Pull the plastic through and cut off excess. Attach tip and match up the strip with the end you want the color to come out of.
6. Begin to pipe. The red will meet up with the thin part of your tip to create the end of the petal color. The red will meet up with the wide end if you want the center to be colored. Move accordingly.

MASTER TIP

As you are piping, you will see where the color is going. You can adjust the 104 tip to make it flow from the wide side or the skinny side. I always give the buttercream a big squeeze before I start to make sure my color is flowing right.

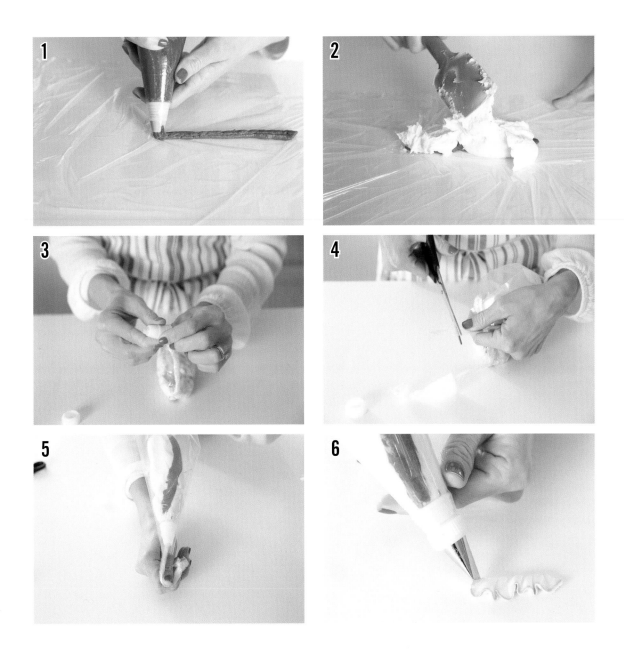

COLORED COCONUT

From the Kitchen	From the Drawer
½ cup shaved sweetened coconut	Small sandwich bag Green food coloring

Instructions

1. Add one large drop of green food coloring to the plastic bag.

2. Add in your shredded coconut and seal bag.

3. Massage the green food coloring into the coconut to color it evenly.

4. This will garnish our Easter basket cookies (page 92).

MASTER TIP

Add pink, yellow, purple, or blue into separate bags to create different colors of straw in the Easter baskets.

GRAHAM CRACKER

From the Kitchen	**From the Drawer**
1 sleeve graham crackers or 8 crackers	Thick plastic bag and rolling pin or food processor Food coloring (optional)

Instructions

1. With a food processor, or thick plastic bag and rolling pin, break up, pulse, and crush the graham crackers into fine crumbs. If you don't want the crumbs to be dyed then stop here.

2. Add three large drops of food coloring to your bag. If using a food processer, add color directly in and mix.

3. Mix up and shake the bag to incorporate all the color into the crumbs. Add more food coloring if needed.

MASTER TIP

The food processor is much easier, but I have used the old *smash the crackers with the rolling pin trick* and you just need to make sure the bag is very thick so it doesn't break open. Do what you can to avoid the mess!

MARBLING SUGAR COOKIES

From the Kitchen
Sugar cookie dough, chilled

From the Drawer
Plastic gloves
Pink, purple, blue, and yellow food
    coloring (or colors of choice)

Instructions

1. Put on gloves, flatten cookie dough, and add food coloring in drops.
2. Mix with hands and gently knead a couple times to mix colors.
3. Roll out dough to ¼-inch thickness.
4. Cut out cookies and bake.

MASTER TIP

The technique can be used for so many occasions. I especially love red and pink marbled hearts for Valentine's Day. Make pink or blue for a baby shower. Get the kids involved and make green shamrocks for St. Patrick's Day.

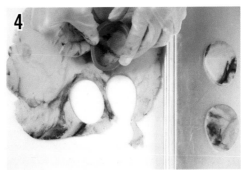

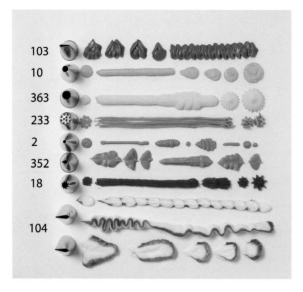

Basic Piping

I use different sizes of each tips. The basics and most used are listed. I provide instructions for each cookie, but use this as a reference if you need more details on a certain style we are piping.

Rosette

To pipe a rosette, use a star tip and hold straight up and down a little off the base of the cookie. Apply pressure and pipe down and then around in a circle and back down to connect. Decrease pressure as you connect, stop pressure, and pull away.

Leaf

Use a leaf tip at a slight 45-degree angle and the two points of the tip will be vertical; I call it the beak because that's what you want it to look like. Squeeze to make a base of the leaf. You will see the buttercream billow out the sides. Slowly pull upward to form the leaf, stop squeezing where you want the leaf to stop, and pull away.

Petal

Hold the bag so the wide end of the tip is at the base of your cookie. The skinny side will be at a 45-degree angle. You will apply pressure and squeeze while rounding your wrist in a half circle to make the petal.

Round Petal

Hold your piping bag so the wide end of the tip is facing away from you and the skinny side is toward you. Hold the piping bag straight up and down, almost touching your base. Squeeze until the buttercream billows out and slowly pull down to create the first petal. Decrease the pressure as you pull down to make the petals shape and stop squeezing.

Ruffle

The wide end of the tip will be touching your cookie base and the skinny end will be facing away from the cookie. Move your wrist up and down slightly to create the first ruffle. Repeat this motion until your ruffle is complete.

Star

Hold the piping bag straight up and the tip just above the surface of the cookie. Squeeze bag to form a star. Use light pressure for a small star and use a lot of pressure to make a larger star. Stop squeezing and then pull up to break the buttercream.

Coloring Buttercream Tips

- I find it easier to mix in small batches at a time. Mix 1 cup to desired shade.
- Generally, use gel food coloring because it is more vibrant, but use liquid food coloring where noted.
- For red, use Wilton's no-taste red gel with crimson/color C in the color right system.
- For white, use Wilton's white-white icing color. (The white in the above photo is dairy-free buttercream. You will notice a slightly different texture.)
- For black buttercream, use super black by Americolor.

- The rest of the colors listed in my instructions can be any brand. I like Wilton and Americolor best.
- Buttercream will darken as it dries after it is piped. To achieve a deep red or super black, add in gel coloring and cover with plastic wrap and allow to sit for a few hours or overnight to darken up.
- When piping with light and dark colors, I'll pipe either the light or dark first and allow to crust over slightly, about an hour before I'll pipe the other color to prevent bleeding.

RECIPES

Recipes

These recipes have been tested and perfected over the years. I've made all the mistakes and changes so you won't have to. I have tried so many buttercream and sugar cookie recipes that I probably should have fallen into a sugar coma by now.

Throughout the years, my sugar cookie recipe has evolved into what my family and I consider the *best* sugar cookie recipe **ever**! Through trial-and-error in my kitchen, I'm sharing my foolproof cookie recipes and my smooth crusting buttercream.

I always use Costco salted sweet cream butter because I think it has the perfect amount of salt in the butter. For authentic The Hutch Oven cookies and buttercream, be sure to use this butter. If you don't have access to that butter, these recipes should work with unsalted butter—but add between ¼ and ½ teaspoon of salt per 1 cup unsalted butter.

I like to roll my cookies out to between ¼-inch and ⅜-inch thick. Nice and thick cookies balance out the sweetness of the buttercream!

CLASSIC SUGAR COOKIE

Makes 24 large cookies

You'll spot both granulated sugar and confectioners' sugar in this recipe. This is because I love the texture of a granulated sugar cookie, but I love the taste of an all-powdered-sugar sugar cookie. This way your cookies stay nice and soft and you get that classic sugar cookie taste. Make sure your baking powder is not expired; this is what gives the cookies their lift. Measure your flour correctly; this will help the cookie keep its shape. These step-by-step photos will help you understand how to measure, cut out, and bake the cookies in my book.

Note*: This recipe is meant to be frosted with my buttercream. If you are looking for a sweeter cookie to just add sprinkles to, add extra vanilla or almond extract to the dough.*

Ingredients
1 cup or 2 sticks salted sweet cream butter
¾ cup white granulated sugar
½ cup white confectioners' sugar
1 large egg
1½ teaspoons pure vanilla extract
3 cups all-purpose flour
1½ teaspoons aluminum-free baking powder

Instructions

1. Cream room-temperature butter in a stand mixer with paddle attachment.

2. Mix in both sugars.

3. Crack your egg in a small bowl to prevent shells in your dough and add into mix.

4. Add in vanilla and cream it all together about 30 seconds on medium speed to fluff the butter and sugars together.

5. Measure flour with spoon method (see page xiv).

6. Mix dry ingredients (flour and baking powder) in a separate bowl with a whisk. Or sift dry ingredients.

7. Add dry ingredients to wet ingredients.

8. Mix on low speed; your dough will seem dry but it will all come together.

9. Preheat oven to 375°F, then cover dough in plastic wrap and refrigerate for at least 15 minutes so dough will firm up a little to prevent spreading. It can also be refrigerated for 10 minutes after the cookies are cut out.

Continued on page 16

. . . Sugar Cookie Continued

10. Flour your surface. I like to press my dough down beforehand to make the surface sticky and then add my flour.

11. Roll out dough to ¼-inch thick.

12. Cut your cookies into desired shapes.

13. Place on a baking sheet, and bake for 6 to 8 minutes or until the cookies puff up.

14. Once baked, let sit for 1 minute on the cookie sheet to firm up. Then transfer to a cooling rack.

15. Perfect sugar cookie!

MASTER TIP

I also to add ¼ teaspoon pure almond extract to my classic cookie recipe sometimes to give it a holiday flavor. Roll your cookies out between ¼ inch and $^3/_8$ of an inch thick; nice and thick cookies balance out the sweetness of the buttercream. I freeze all my cookies for at least two hours or overnight before I even frost them because it makes them softer. Frosted cookies can also be frozen for a week or two before event. If you want to freeze them, you can place a piece of parchment paper between cookie layers. When you pull them out of the freezer, be sure to unstack them right away to allow the buttercream to crust back over. I treat my cookies like I would a cupcake and lay them in a single layer in a box or on a tray until they are ready to stack.

No-Chill Cookie Recipe

This will work on all cookies using regular butter. Dairy-free option needs to be chilled longer.

1. Preheat oven to 375°F.

2. Cut cold butter into 1-inch cubes, add to mixer, and mix for 1 minute until creamy.

3. Add in both sugars and mix until incorporated, about 1 to 2 minutes.

4. Add in rest of wet ingredients and mix again for 1 minute.

5. Continue steps 5 through 15, but leave out step 9.

MASTER TIP

Roll out cookies to ¼ inch to prevent them from over-crisping. The thinner the cookie, the faster they will brown and crisp. If you make them thinner, watch the baking time. Bake until just puffed up and then remove from oven. This is usually 6 to 7 minutes, but know your oven because temperature can be tricky. Freeze unfrosted cookies for 2 hours or overnight before frosting to make them softer.

BROWN-SUGAR COOKIE

Makes 24 large cookies

This recipe is a brown-sugar cookie—not a sugar cookie that happens to be brown. These soft, delicious cookies have a rich brown-sugar flavor with a slightly crisp edge. They remind me of a chocolate chip cookie without the chocolate but still hold their shape to decorate on. I think it's fun to play with different things in the kitchen to see what works and what doesn't. I loved how this recipe came out, but I needed to be sure it wasn't just me, so I brought a batch of these cookies to a girl's lunch and the mmm's and heads nodding in agreement were all I needed to assure me this was a hit! I think it's important to bring in your squad of cookie-loving friends to help you with decisions, such as: does brown sugar work in a cookie? Verdict? YES!!

Ingredients
1 cup or 2 sticks salted sweet cream butter
1 cup packed brown sugar
1½ teaspoons vanilla extract
1 pinch salt
1 egg
3 cups flour
1½ teaspoons aluminum-free baking powder

Instructions

1. Cream butter, brown sugar, vanilla, pinch of salt, and egg together in a stand mixer on medium speed for about 30 seconds to 1 minute.

2. Mix dry ingredients (flour and baking powder) in separate bowl. I use a whisk to blend the dry ingredients together.

3. Add dry ingredients to your wet ingredients. Mix until the cookie mix becomes a dough and it pulls away from the sides of the bowl. It will seem a little dry, but it will all come together.

4. Remove dough from bowl, wrap in plastic, and place in the fridge for at least 15 minutes. If you flatten the dough, it gets colder quicker. This will allow your dough to firm up a bit for rolling and getting sharp edges. You can also roll out cookies, place them on a baking sheet, and refrigerate for 10 minutes.

5. Preheat oven to 375°F while your dough chills.

6. Flour your surface and roll out dough to ¼-inch thick. Cut out your cookies into desired shapes.

7. Place on a baking sheet, and bake for 6 to 7 minutes or just until the cookies puff up. These will brown faster than your regular sugar cookies.

8. Once baked, let sit for 1 minute on the cookie sheet to firm up.

9. Transfer to a cooling rack so they can cool completely.

CHOCOLATE CHIP CUT-OUT COOKIES

Makes 24 large cookies

My love for chocolate chip cookies and sugar cookies collided and one delicious cookie was made. I wanted a rich chocolate chip cookie taste without the dough spreading. They stay soft as long as you don't overbake them. Truly this is one of my favorite cookies. You can finely chop up dark chocolate and add that in place of the semi-sweet minis. These cookies have quickly become a family favorite. We love chocolate chip cookies.

Ingredients

1 cup or 2 sticks salted sweet cream butter
1 cup packed brown sugar
1½ teaspoons vanilla extract
1 pinch salt

1 egg
3 cups flour
1½ teaspoons aluminum-free baking powder
½ cup mini semisweet chocolate chips

Instructions

1. Cream butter, brown sugar, vanilla, pinch of salt, and egg together in a stand mixer on medium speed for about 30 seconds to 1 minute.

2. Mix dry ingredients (flour and baking powder) in a separate bowl. I use a whisk to blend the dry ingredients together.

3. Add dry ingredients to your wet ingredients. Mix until the cookie mix becomes a dough and it pulls away from the sides of the bowl. It will seem a little dry, but it will all come together.

4. Add in mini chocolate chips and mix again.

5. Remove dough from bowl, wrap in plastic, and place in fridge for at least 15 minutes. If you flatten the dough, it gets colder quicker. Preheat oven to 375°F while your dough chills.

6. Flour your surface and roll out dough to ¼-inch thick. Cut your cookies into desired shapes.

7. Place on a baking sheet, and bake for 6 to 7 minutes or just until the cookie puffs up. These will brown faster than your regular sugar cookies. Don't overbake—we want these soft, like chocolate chip cookies.

8. Once baked, let sit for 1 minute on the cookie sheet to firm up. Transfer to a cooling rack so they can cool completely.

MASTER TIP

I suggest using aluminum-free baking powder because it's a double acting leavening agent that reacts when liquid and heat are added.

MASTER TIP

Make sure to keep the cookies thick because you want a soft cookie. Thinner rolled cookies crisp faster in the oven. Cut these with a scalloped cookie cutter for Valentine's day. Freeze unfrosted cookies for 2 hours or overnight before frosting to make them softer.

RED VELVET SUGAR COOKIES

Makes 24 large cookies

I have dreamed of a cookie like this. I can't even tell you how many batches I had to throw out and tweak to get them perfect. Make these for any holiday or birthday, because red velvet shouldn't just be for Valentine's Day. I used red velvet emulsion that I ordered online for this recipe.

Ingredients

1 cup or 2 sticks salted sweet cream butter
¾ cup white granulated sugar
½ cup confectioners' sugar
1 teaspoon vanilla extract
1 tablespoon red velvet emulsion
½ teaspoon white distilled vinegar

1 large egg
2 tablespoons unsweetened cocoa powder
3 cups all-purpose flour
1 pinch salt
1½ teaspoons aluminum-free baking powder

Instructions

1. Cream butter, sugars, vanilla, red velvet emulsion, vinegar, and egg together in a stand mixer on medium speed for 1 minute.

2. Mix dry ingredients (cocoa powder, flour, pinch of salt, and baking powder) in a separate bowl. I use a whisk to blend the dry ingredients together.

3. Add dry ingredients to your wet ingredients. Mix until the cookie mix becomes a dough and it pulls away from the sides of the bowl.

4. Preheat oven to 375°F.

5. Remove dough from bowl, wrap in plastic, and place in fridge for at least 15 minutes. If you flatten the dough, it gets colder quicker. This will allow your dough to firm up a bit for rolling and helps prevent spreading.

6. Flour your surface or use some cocoa powder to roll your cookies; most of the flour will bake off.

7. Roll out dough to ¼-inch thick. Cut your cookies into desired shapes.

8. Place on a baking sheet, and bake for 6 to 7 minutes or until the cookies puff up. These cookies will bake fast and they won't brown since the cookie is deep red.

9. Once baked, let sit for 1 minute on the cookie sheet to firm up. Transfer to a cooling rack.

CHOCOLATE SUGAR COOKIES

Makes 24 large cookies

It's no secret that I love cookies, and I really love chocolate, so naturally we are bringing it into the kitchen. These chocolate cookies hold their shape perfectly and have just the right amount of chocolate. They remind me of little brownies. You can decorate them with buttercream or shake powdered sugar over them. I think chocolate ghost shaped cookies with powdered sugar would be a darling Halloween treat.

Ingredients
1 cup or 2 sticks salted sweet cream butter
¾ cup granulated white sugar
½ cup confectioners' sugar
1½ teaspoons vanilla extract
1 pinch salt
1 large egg
½ cup unsweetened cocoa powder
2⅔ cups flour
1½ teaspoons aluminum-free baking powder

Instructions

1. Cream butter, sugars, vanilla, pinch of salt, and egg together in a stand mixer on medium speed for 1 minute.

2. Mix dry ingredients (cocoa powder, flour, and baking powder) in a separate bowl. I use a whisk to blend the dry ingredients together.

3. Add dry ingredients to your wet ingredients. Mix until the cookie mix becomes a dough and it pulls away from the sides of the bowl.

4. Preheat oven to 375°F degrees.

5. Remove dough from bowl, wrap in plastic, and place in fridge for at least 15 minutes. If you flatten the dough, it gets colder quicker. This will allow your dough to firm up a bit for rolling and getting sharp edges.

6. Flour your surface or use some cocoa powder to roll your cookies; the flour will bake off.

7. Roll out dough to ¼-inch thick. Cut your cookies into desired shapes.

8. Place on a baking sheet, and bake for 6 to 7 minutes or until the cookies puff up. These cookies will bake fast and they won't brown since the cookie is already brown, so it can be tricky. When they puff up on the tops, this normally means they are done enough to come out. If you overcook these, they can get hard.

9. Once baked, let sit for 1 minute on the cookie sheet to firm up. Transfer to a cooling rack.

DAIRY-FREE SUGAR COOKIES

Makes 24 large cookies

My sister is dairy free so making a cookie she can eat was important to me. I love when the whole family can bake, decorate, and eat. It's so sad when someone gets left out because of their allergies.

I've tried a few different types of dairy-free butter substitutes but they didn't taste right. My friend is DF, as well, and she suggested I use the Earth Balance Soy-Free Buttery Spread and it worked brilliantly. Keep the spread cold, and don't let it get to room temperature before using or the dough will be too sticky.

Ingredients

1 cup cold Earth Balance Soy-Free Buttery Spread
¾ cup white granulated sugar
½ cup white confectioners' sugar
1½ teaspoons vanilla extract

1 large egg
3 cups flour plus extra for rolling
1½ teaspoons aluminum-free baking powder

Instructions

1. Cream Earth Balance spread, both sugars, vanilla, and egg together for 1 minute on medium speed.
2. Mix dry ingredients (flour and baking powder) in a separate bowl. I use a whisk to blend the dry ingredients together, but you can sift the dry ingredients together if that's preferable.
3. Add dry ingredients to your wet ingredients. Mix until the cookie mix becomes a dough and it pulls away from the sides of the bowl.
4. Remove dough from bowl, wrap in plastic, and place in the fridge for at least 20 minutes. This will allow your dough to firm up a bit for rolling and getting sharp edges. The soy-free spread will make the dough soft, so more chill time is necessary.
5. Preheat oven to 375°F.
6. Flour surface and roll out dough to ¼-inch thick. Cut your cookies into desired shapes.
7. Place on a baking sheet, and bake for 6 to 7 minutes or until the cookies puff up.
8. Once baked, let sit for 5 minutes on the cookie sheet to firm up. Transfer to a cooling rack.
9. Freeze cookies at least 2 hours or overnight

MASTER TIP

If you ever have a problem with cookies rising, add an extra teaspoon of baking powder. Make vegan using 1 tablespoon ground flaxseed meal and 3 tablespoons water. Let sit for 5 minutes before adding egg replacement.

GLUTEN-FREE SUGAR COOKIE RECIPE

Makes 24 large cookies

Some of my closest friends cannot have gluten. I really wanted to include everyone in this book. I know it's especially hard when your children cannot have gluten, so this recipe allows the whole family to be included—everyone can eat the cookies. This is a gluten-free recipe that doesn't spread and stays soft. I have found that the 1 to 1 flour is easy and so handy. I'm excited to share a delicious recipe that is simple, special, and so yummy! Put on your apron and let's get to it.

Ingredients

1 cup or 2 sticks salted sweet cream butter
¾ cup white granulated sugar
½ cup white confectioners' sugar
1½ teaspoons pure gluten-free vanilla extract
1 large egg
2¾ cups 1-to-1 gluten-free flour, plus extra for rolling
1½ teaspoons aluminum-free baking powder

Instructions

1. Cream butter, both sugars, vanilla, and egg together for 1 minute on medium speed.
2. Mix dry ingredients (flour and baking powder) in a separate bowl. I use a whisk to blend the dry ingredients together. You can also sift the dry ingredients together.
3. Add dry ingredients to your wet ingredients. Mix until the cookie mix becomes a dough and it pulls away from the sides of the bowl. It will seem a little dry, but it will all come together.
4. Remove dough from bowl, wrap in plastic, and place in the fridge for at least 15 minutes. This will allow your dough to firm up a bit for rolling and getting sharp edges.
5. Preheat oven to 375°F.
6. Flour your surface and roll out dough to ¼-inch thick. Cut your cookies into desired shapes.
7. Place on a baking sheet, and bake for 6 to 7 minutes or until the cookies puff up. Cookie will dry out quickly if you overbake with the gluten-free flour.
8. Let cool on a cookie sheet for around 5 minutes or the cookie can crumble. Transfer to a cooling rack.

MASTER TIP

Keep your cookies soft by freezing them for an hour or overnight. When you retrieve your cookies from the freezer, make sure they are thawed before you frost.

GLUTEN-FREE AND DAIRY-FREE SUGAR COOKIE

Makes 24 large cookies

Don't let your allergies stop you from being able to make a delicious and beautiful sugar cookie. I have removed dairy and gluten from this sugar cookie recipe and tweaked it so they aren't dry. I know how limited good and tasty recipes are when they have to be GF and DF. I was really excited when I got this cookie just right; I know some special people who can't eat cookies because of their health restrictions, and I wanted to change that—I wanted them to be able to eat all the cookies! Now you can create special memories with your whole family using this recipe, and no one gets left out.

Ingredients
1 cup cold Earth Balance Soy-Free Buttery Spread
¾ cup white granulated sugar
½ cup white confectioners' sugar
1½ teaspoons vanilla extract
1 large egg
3 cups Bob's Red Mill 1 to 1 flour, plus extra for rolling
1½ teaspoons aluminum-free baking powder

Instructions

1. Cream Earth Balance spread, both sugars, vanilla, and egg together for 1 minute on medium speed.

2. Mix dry ingredients (flour and baking powder) in separate bowl. I use a whisk to blend the dry ingredients together, but you can sift them.

3. Add dry ingredients to your wet ingredients. Mix until the cookie mix becomes a dough.

4. This dough will be sticky, so put the bowl in the refrigerator for 20 to 30 minutes. This will allow your dough to firm up a bit for rolling. The soy-free spread will make the dough soft, so more chill time is necessary.

5. Preheat oven to 375°F.

6. Flour surface and very gently roll out dough to ¼-inch thick. Cut your cookies into desired shapes.

7. Place on a baking sheet, and bake for 6 to 7 minutes or when the cookies puff up.

8. Once baked, let sit for 5 minutes on the cookie sheet to firm up. Transfer to a cooling rack.

MASTER TIP

Make sure to follow instructions and ingredients. Bob's Red Mill 1 to 1 flour works perfectly. The Earth Balance Soy-Free Buttery Spread in the little red tubs doesn't have a funny aftertaste like the sticks do. The spread needs to come right out of the fridge when using, otherwise the dough is too sticky.

BUTTERCREAM BASICS

You *can* frost cookies with buttercream and they won't get completely smashed when stacking—it's true! For this recipe, you cut the butter with vegetable-based shortening to form a crust; however, they can still be smashed if a lot of pressure is applied. I treat them like cupcakes and don't stack them until the last minute.

I like my buttercream for piping to be nice and smooth. You will see in the directions that I only mix for a minute or two. Overmixing causes the buttercream to become a bit grainy with tiny air bubbles. We want a nice and smooth consistency. You can still add your food colorings after mixing; this will not ruin the buttercream. I like to add food coloring in small batches, so I mix a cup or two at a time. Find what works best for you.

You will use this recipe throughout the book when your ingredient list calls for a "batch of buttercream."

Note: This will not be hard like a royal icing. Read the Master Tips at the end of this recipe before adding in heavy cream.

MASTER TIPS

I highly (highly) suggest you use Costco sweet cream salted butter. If you don't have that, Lucerne also has a great sweet cream butter that has the right amount of salt. If you want to, use unsalted butter then add ¼ teaspoon of salt when you are creaming butter and shortening.

I've made this recipe a million times, and the weather is a huge factor. When it's hot out, I use half the cream, and when it's cold, I use the full amount plus extra. If 3 tablespoons is not enough, slowly add in 1 tablespoon at a time to achieve desired consistency. After you make this once, you'll find how much cream or milk works with your climate. The temperature of your house, and humidity of where you live, will determine how much milk to add. Start out with the minimum and slowly add to find out what works best for you.

Make sure your shortening is fresh and not left in a warm spot. It develops a yucky taste over time, and we don't want that. Add in 1 teaspoon of meringue powder; it helps thicken buttercream if you are in a hotter climate.

Use a 2-pound bag of powdered sugar plus 1 and ½ cups to make life easier so you don't have to measure 9 cups of powdered sugar each time.

After piping your buttercream, allow 6 to 8 hours to dry the crust before stacking.

CRUSTING AMERICAN BUTTERCREAM

Makes about 4 cups

This recipe works best for me for decorating. It's a little sweet but the powdered sugar makes a strong crust. You can use all butter and it will still form a crust; however, the shortening gives it a smoother texture. Typically for a buttercream recipe you would mix until light and fluffy, but not this recipe. You want the buttercream to be nice and smooth, so we will just mix for a minute or two. This was adapted from Wilton's buttercream recipe. You can add either heavy cream or milk; I like the thickness that heavy cream provides to the buttercream. Milk will just make for a thinner buttercream which may help in colder climates.

Ingredients

1 cup salted sweet cream butter, room temperature
1 cup Crisco shortening, room temperature
2 teaspoons vanilla extract
9 cups confectioners' sugar
3 tablespoons heavy cream or milk

Instructions

1. Cream your butter and shortening until well incorporated. Both must be at room temperature to prevent clumping.

2. Once creamed, add your vanilla. Mix again for 1 minute.

3. Sift your powdered sugar to make sure there are no clumps and add it in.

4. Place a towel over your mixer to prevent a powdered sugar storm.

5. Once mixed, slowly add in your heavy cream or milk, 1 tablespoon at a time (you can always add more but you can't take it out). Continue to add more than the recipe states if it's too thick.

6. Mix until smooth, about 1 minute on medium to high speed. Be sure not to overwhip your buttercream. DON'T panic—you won't ruin it if it whips longer. Store unused buttercream in an airtight container in the fridge for up to a week or freeze for up to three months.

DAIRY-FREE BUTTERCREAM

Makes about 4 cups

This buttercream will pair with the dairy-free cookie recipe. I have tested this recipe on people with and without dairy allergies and everyone loves it. It tastes sweet, creamy, and delicious so no one will even know you don't have butter in it. It will form a very thin crust just like the original buttercream because we are adding in a lot of confectioners' sugar. Allow 6 to 8 hours before stacking for the crust to form.

Ingredients

1 cup Earth Balance Soy-Free Buttery Spread in the tub, room temperature
1 cup vegetable shortening
2 teaspoons pure vanilla extract
9 cups confectioners' sugar
1–3 tablespoons vanilla almond milk

Instructions

1. Mix spread and shortening together in a stand mixer.

2. Add in vanilla extract.

3. Mix in powdered sugar.

4. Add in almond milk one tablespoon at a time. You can always add more in if it's too thick.

5. Mix until smooth, about 1 minute on medium to high speed. Be sure not to overwhip your buttercream. DON'T panic—you won't ruin it if it whips longer. Store unused buttercream in an airtight container in the fridge for up to a week or freeze for up to three months.

MASTER TIP

The amount of almond milk will vary. The temperature of your house and humidity of where you live will determine how much to add. Start out with the minimum and slowly add to find out what works best for you. Make sure your shortening is fresh and not left in a warm spot. It develops a yucky taste over time and we don't want that. Add in extra powdered sugar if the buttercream is not crusting enough.

FLAVORED BUTTERCREAM

Makes about 4 cups

I love the thought of fresh fruit in my recipes. I know that some bakers will say to use freeze-dried berries in their buttercream, and that's fine too. I will explain how to use freeze-dried strawberries and raspberries in the master tip section. It really is just personal preference. You can use a blackberry, strawberry, or raspberry for this recipe. I don't recommend using blueberries.

I like to add in a couple drops of lemon essential oil to give the lemon buttercream a boost of flavor, too.

BERRY BUTTERCREAM	LEMON BUTTERCREAM
Ingredients	**Ingredients**
1 cup or 2 sticks sweet cream butter, room temperature	1 cup or 2 sticks of sweet cream butter, room temperature
1 cup vegetable shortening	1 cup vegetable shortening
1 teaspoon pure vanilla extract	1 teaspoon pure vanilla extract
2 tablespoons crushed berries or ½ cup freeze dried berries	1 tablespoon fresh squeezed lemon juice
9 cups confectioners' sugar	½ teaspoon very finely grated lemon zest
1–3 tablespoons heavy cream	9 cups confectioners' or white powdered sugar
	1–3 tablespoons heavy cream

Instructions

1. Cream your room temperature butter and shortening on medium speed for 1 minute.

2. Once creamed, add your vanilla and crushed berries OR lemon juice and zest. Mix again for 1 minute.

3. Sift your powdered sugar to make sure there are no clumps and add it to the bowl.

4. Place a towel over your mixer to prevent a powdered sugar storm.

5. Once mixed, slowly add in your heavy cream; remember, you can always add more but you can't take it out.

6. Mix until smooth, about 1 to 2 minutes on medium to high speed. This buttercream can be mixed a little longer if necessary. Store unused buttercream in an airtight container in the fridge for up to a week or freeze for up to three months.

MASTER TIP

Fruit can cause the buttercream to sweat. Add extra powdered sugar if you feel like the buttercream needs to be thicker. Add in more heavy cream if too thick.

For freeze dried option, pulse ½ cup freeze dried berries in a food processor. The berries will become a powder. Add that powder into your buttercream instead of the fresh berries.

HONEY GLAZE

As soon as I made this glaze, my kids wanted to join in and help. I love decorating in the kitchen with my kids; Reese and I had so much fun making galaxy cookies. We added tiny gold stars after we dipped them. To make galaxy glaze, add blue, black, purple, and pink food coloring. There are so many possibilities, and it's fun to come up with new ideas with your kids because they get so creative with their colors. These cookies were made with lots of laughs and a ton of love.

Drizzle, dip, pour, or flood this yummy glaze over your cookies. Let it set for 1 to 2 hours or overnight. For plain glazed cookies, leave out step 6. This the glaze I refer to throughout the book for marbling, so I've included those instructions here, as well.

Ingredients
½ tablespoon honey
2 tablespoons milk plus 2 teaspoons
1 teaspoon clear vanilla extract
½ teaspoon lemon juice
2¼ cups confectioners' sugar

Instructions

1. Mix honey and milk together in a medium bowl.

2. Add clear vanilla and keep stirring.

3. Add lemon juice. I know it sounds strange but it balances out the sweetness

4. Sift your confectioners' sugar to make sure there are no clumps and add it to the bowl.

5. You should be able to pull the spoon straight up and it will drizzle down.

For marbling, continue as follows.

6. Put a drop of liquid food coloring in glaze and gently swirl. Don't overmix.

Continued on page 38

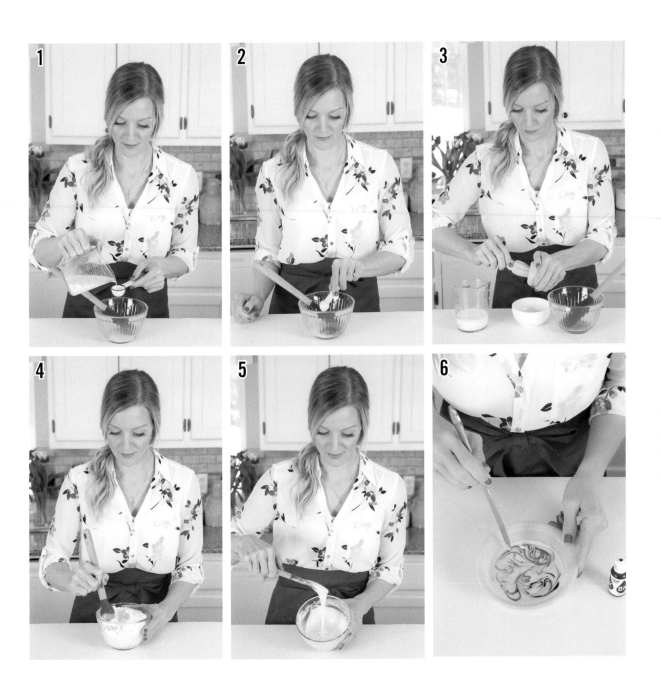

...Honey Glaze Continued

7. Dip cookie straight down into glaze until its fully coated. Don't swirl cookie.

8. Pull straight up and let the glaze drip off for a second and quickly flip over.

9. Pop any air bubbles with a toothpick or knife tip. Place on wire rack with parchment paper to catch any drips. Allow 2 hours to dry. Overnight for best results.

MASTER TIP

You can use 1 tablespoon of honey, if desired (my son prefers less honey).

Mix in any colors to marbleize your cookies. Liquid food coloring will work best in marbling cookies because it's thinner and can be swirled through the glaze with ease.

Another option is to outline with buttercream and fill with glaze. Your glaze will dry harder than your buttercream because the buttercream just crusts over.

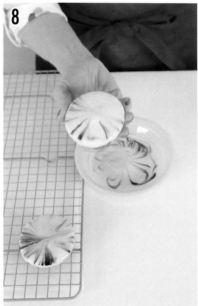

Winter

Luke 2:11 Today in the town of David a Savior has been born to you; he is the Messiah, the Lord.

Traditions in our family have always been so important. Now that I have my own family, I'm even more set on keeping traditions alive. One thing we do every year is what we call the Denali Express (in years past, it's been the Navigator Express; it just depends on the vehicle we have). We drive around looking at Christmas lights and watch *The Polar Express* movie. We surprise the kids with new pajamas, bags of popcorn, and hot chocolate. They get to wear a bell around their necks and they hold a ticket that I punch every year. It's fun to count up the punches to see how long we've been doing it. Now, as my kids have gotten older, there has been some eyerolling here and there, which I naturally ignore. I've always told them they will appreciate the memories someday. Well this year, as Reese doesn't have much time in the house before she goes off to college, the kids excitedly listed all our traditions off to make sure we didn't forget one. Christmas cookies are always a tradition that I have NEVER had an eyeroll

over. I hope these cookies help you and your family start a new tradition or perhaps level-up a tradition already in place.

For our family, celebrating the birth of Jesus is important. Going to church and gathering is beautiful, and I especially enjoy the candlelight Christmas Eve service. That is another tradition I hope my children carry with them.

Make cookie decorating fun and easy. I give two different colors of buttercream to everyone with a couple different tips attached to make lots of different designs. (The star tip is one kids take well to.) They can make their own designs. I add a few different sprinkles in a cupcake tin with liners to make disposal easy because you can add the left-over sprinkles back into containers when finished. Keep an angled spatula handy so you can smooth out the buttercream if mistakes are made, creating a new canvas to pipe on.

Hat & Mittens
page 46

page 50

cookies

Rudolph & His Red Nose

page 53

HAT & MITTENS

Is there anything more adorable than little hat and mitten cookies? The temperature drops and the sweaters come out. I love beanie and scarf weather. My daughter says this might be her favorite cookie in the book.

From the Kitchen

Hat- and mitten-shaped cookies
Batch of buttercream
Cup of hot water

From the Drawer

Angled spatula
Clear sugar crystals
Tips 12, 363, 2 or 3, 1A
White food coloring

Hat Instructions

1. Using tip 12, outline the hat but do not frost to the very edge (see picture).

2. Use my smooth buttercream technique on the hat for the base of the frosting. See on page 3.

3. Attach tip 363, start at the top, and do a crisscross pattern to the base of the hat. Make sure to keep the very bottom clear; we're going to add to it.

4. Attach tip 3 and make two lines side by side like a ladder. Make a crisscross pattern so it has an almost braided look. Do this to the right and left sides of the center braid we just completed.

5. With tip 363, make two smaller crisscrosses on the very outside on both the right and the left.

6. Turn the cookie vertical; we are going to pipe the brim of the hat. With tip 363 attached, pipe in a crisscross pattern all the way down to the border just under the hat.

7. Turn the cookie upside down and, with tip 1A, make a big dollop of buttercream for the pompom on the top of the hat.

8. On that pompom, add come clear sugar crystals.

Mittens on page 48.

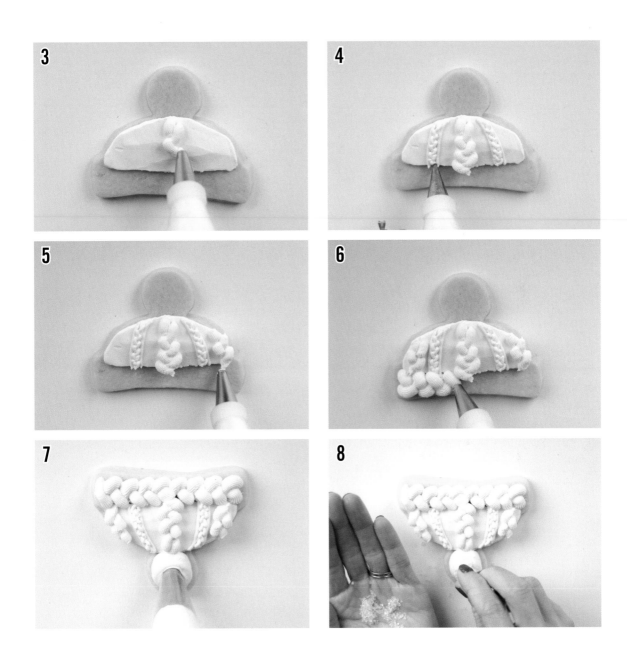

Mitten Instructions

1. Use tip 12 with white buttercream and outline the cookie, but leave room to line the mitten.

2. Use my smooth buttercream technique (page 3).

3. Attach tip 363 and on the cuff of the cookie that we left blank make a crisscross pattern down, making small overlapping X's with the buttercream. Have your piping bag angled toward you at a 45-degree angle.

4. Start piping at the top of the mitten down to the cuff with the same crisscross pattern. Use less pressure to make the pattern smaller.

5. Move to the part where the thumb begins and create another braided crisscross pattern down to the cuff.

6. Attach tip 2 and start in between the two braids we just made on the mitten. Make two vertical lines close together like a ladder. Pipe in that same crisscross motion all the way down. We are overlapping a tiny bit to create that knitted look. Pipe on the far right and far left sides of the mitten.

MASTER TIPS

I think these would be so darling in any color; feel free to get creative! You can also make the braided parts a shade darker to add dimension to the cookie. Practice doing the braided look on a napkin or paper plate to gain confidence before beginning on the smooth buttercream.

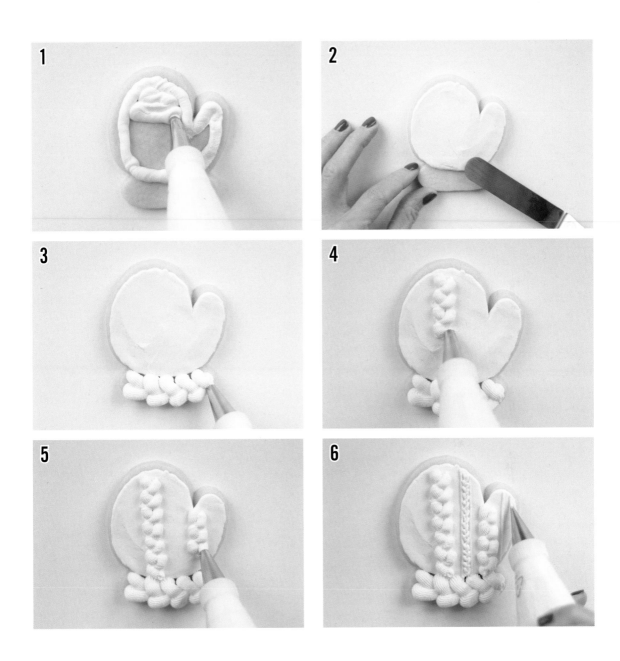

POINSETTIA & HOLLY

These are easily one of my favorite cookies. My mother always had a beautiful poinsettia on the table at our holiday dinners. I recently learned from an expert that the petals of the poinsettia aren't even the petals—the red, white, and pink/white petals are actually leaves and the flower is the center clusters.

From the Kitchen	From the Drawer
Round- and holly-shaped cookies	Gold nonpareils or sugar pearls
Batch of buttercream	Tips 366, 352, 12, and 5
	Red, white, and green gel food coloring

Poinsettia Instructions

1. Use tip 366 with your red buttercream. I added some white to mine using the two-toned buttercream technique (page 4). Hold your beak or pointed end of the tip facing down. Slightly angle your piping bag so it's not straight up and down. Squeeze a large amount of buttercream in the outer edge of the cookie, but not the very edge—you want to be able to turn the cookie before you start moving the bag back. Slowly pull it back while gently squeezing.

2. Repeat this all the way around the cookie, leaving a little room for the center leaves.

3. Make the center leaves using the same piping technique, but this time we aren't going to pipe long leaves because they will just fill in the middle.

4. Add the gold sugar pearls to the center for the flower.

5. Use green and tip 352 to make the outer green leaves of your poinsettia.

6. Between each red leaf, add a green one to pull the cookie together.

Holly on page 52

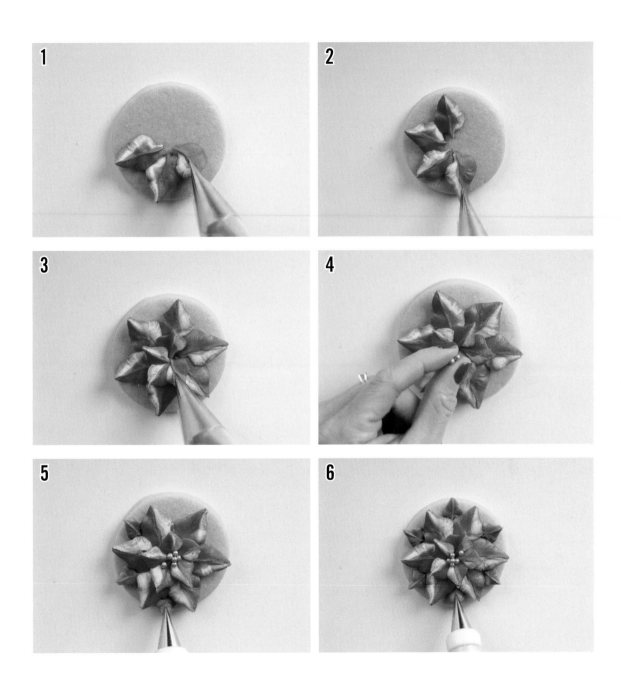

Holly Instructions

1. Outline your holly cookie with tip 5 and your green buttercream. Don't pipe to the very edge because we love to see that pretty cookie underneath.

2. Once outlined, you will fill in the holly. Pipe back and forth horizontally until you've filled the cookie. I pipe with my bag tilted toward me, so the buttercream flows out more like a tube rather than flat.

3. Pipe a vein down the center from the top all the way down to the bottom.

4. Use tip 12 and the red buttercream to make the holly berries. Hold your piping bag close to the cookie but not touching. Gently squeeze until the buttercream billows out the sides and stop. Wait to pull up on your berry until after you stop squeezing so it makes it clean and not a pointed end.

MASTER TIPS

I love to make white poinsettias, pink and white, red and white, or just red. They look beautiful even if you don't add the green to the outer layer of leaves. The holly can be piped on a round cookie as well.

RUDOLPH & HIS RED NOSE

This is a perfect plate of cookies for Santa. The kids can easily help you with these. Get creative and make them your own. It would be fun to make all the reindeer for the sleigh and put them together on a plate. You can find reindeer cookie cutters online, and even if they don't look the same, you can use this technique. I can personally guarantee that Santa will LOVE these cookies.

From the Kitchen	**From the Drawer**
Reindeer- and round-shaped cookies	Angled spatula
Batch of buttercream	Tips 10, 103, 2
Cup of hot water	Brown, red, and black gel food coloring

Rudolph's Red Nose Nose Instructions

1. Use tip 10 and your red buttercream to fill the cookie but don't pipe to the very edge.
2. Use my smooth buttercream technique on page 3.

Rudolph on page 54

Rudolph Instructions

1. Using tip 103 with the wide side of the tip facing the outside of your cookie, start squeezing until the buttercream billows out. Slowly pull back from the first part of the antler. Add three more antlers to complete each side. You are basically drawing with the tip. Your bag should be straight up and down, ⅛ of an inch from the cookie.

2. Make the ears by turning the tip so the skinny side is facing outward and the fat side is facing you. Pipe in a round motion with your wrist to make the ear look like a deer ear.

3. Attach tip 10 to outline and fill the cookie.

4. Use my smooth buttercream technique (page 3).

5. Use tip 10 with red buttercream to pipe the nose. Hold piping bag close to the cookie to add a big dollop.

6. Attach tip 2 to the black buttercream to add two little eyes above the nose. Add a little crooked smile with the same black.

MASTER TIPS

Practice on a paper plate or paper towel before you move onto the cookie. Add some edible glitter or red sanding sugar to Rudolph's nose to make it shine. Add in some peppermint extract for a festive flavor to your buttercream before piping. A round tip would also work great for the antlers.

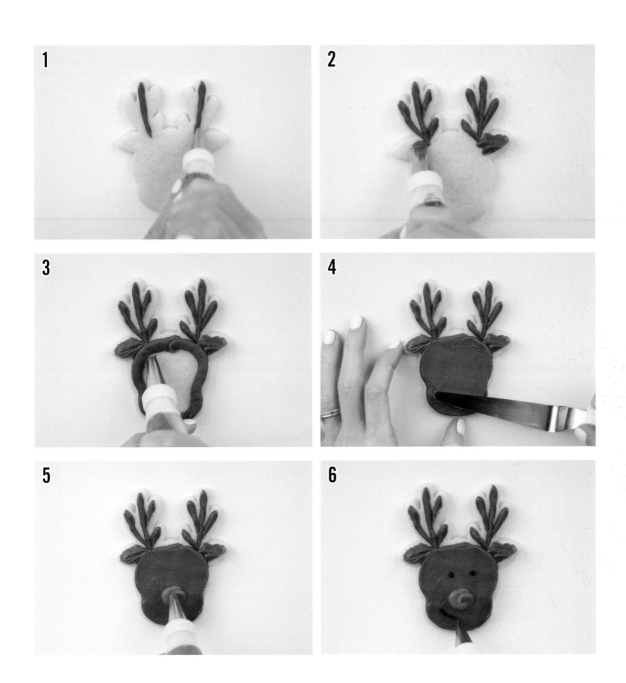

Winter Wonderland

page 58

Mistletoe

page 64

WINTER WONDERLAND

This plate represents all-things Winter with the snowflake, tree, and the wreaths. Have you ever been to a wreath-making workshop, or made wreaths with your friends? Turn them into cookie form and the possibilities are endless. For the wreaths, I use a scalloped circle and a mini cookie cutter to cut out the center. Let's begin to frost our Winter Wonderland!

From the Kitchen
Tree-, snowflake-, and round scalloped-
shaped circle cookies with a hole in
the center
Batch of buttercream

From the Drawer
Sugar crystals
Red and white nonpareils or sugar pearls
Tips 21, 17, 4, 233, and 352
Red, white, and green gel food coloring

Tree Instructions

1. We will use tip 17 and green buttercream for this cookie. Start piping on the bottom layer of your tree, but at the top of that layer, as pictured. Squeeze the buttercream with your bag angled toward you to make the branches skinny and full. Pipe in one steady stream to the bottom of your layer. Continue to do this as you cover that bottom layer of your tree.

2. On the second layer, we will pipe the same technique but start in the middle of the tree.

3. Continue to pipe the branches until the second layer is covered in buttercream.

4. For the top layer, we will have to overlap a couple of the branches at the point of our tree. Keep piping; there should be four branches at the top.

5. Last, sprinkle your white nonpareils or sugar pearls just under the top layer and middle layer of branches to make snow.

6. Completed Winter Wonderland tree.

MASTER TIPS

Change up the colors on the snowflakes; pastel would be pretty. Add sugar crystals in place of the white nonpareils or edible confetti glitter for the snow. Add colorful lights on your tree with tip 4 and pipe different colors down a buttercream string. Add a star to the very top for a decorated Christmas tree. Make the tree and wreath flocked by adding white buttercream into your green buttercream using the two-toned method on page 4.

Snowflake on page 60
Wreath with Red Berries on page 62
Wreath with Holly on page 62

Snowflake Instructions

1. Use tip 21 and white buttercream to frost your snowflake. Start at the top point and squeeze the buttercream in a steady stream, slowly moving the tip back and forth to make a slight wave all the way down to the opposite tip at the bottom while holding your bag at a 45-degree angle.

2. Pipe on the rest of the snowflake from the center out to the tips in the same motion.

3. Continue until the snowflake is filled.

4. Dip your cookie face-down gently in a bowl of clear sugar crystals to coat the cookie and make it sparkly.

5. With our red buttercream and tip 4, make a dollop at the tip of one end and slowly move the piping bag toward the middle. Ease up on the pressure as you go to make a small design. This will make it skinnier as it ends. We are drawing on our snowflake.

6. Continue this around each tip of the snowflake.

7. Now attach tip 4 to your white buttercream and make a design on both sides of the red. Instead of pulling straight down, you will make your dollop and move inward toward the red buttercream you have already piped.

8. Continue to do this on both sides of the red, all the way around your cookie, making a beautiful and easy design. Finish it off with a dollop of red in the center of the snowflake.

Wreath with Red Berries Instructions

1. Use tip 352 and your light green buttercream. We will be piping leaves all around this wreath. Make sure the beak of the tip is facing down in a point, as pictured. Start piping on one end of the cookie.

2. Squeeze for about ½ inch, making a little wave motion with your piping bag to create dimension in the leaves, and stop. Angle your bag toward you to create the leaves. The longer you squeeze, the longer the leaves will be. Keep making layers until you have filled the whole cookie with a desired amount of buttercream leaves/branches.

3. Use about 15 red nonpareils, spreading them in clusters of three around the wreath to create little holly berries.

Wreath with Holly Instructions

1. Use tip 233 and light green buttercream. Pipe the buttercream around the cookie in a clockwise motion, all the way around. Your piping tip will be straight up and down about ¼ inch off the cookie.

2. Make two or three layers of this buttercream, and slowly move the piping bag up further off the cookie so you don't smash what you have already piped.

3. With tip 352 and a darker shade of buttercream, pipe the holly leaves at the top or bottom of the cookie. Make sure the beak of the tip is facing down, as pictured. Squeeze out the buttercream and slowly pull back and then stop squeezing where you want the leaf to end.

4. Pipe three holly leaves in a cluster.

5. Next, using tip 4 and red buttercream, pipe three holly berries in the center of the leaves.

6. Finish off the wreath with some clear sugar crystals to give it a holiday look.

MISTLETOE

Kiss under a cookie mistletoe! My husband is my person, so it was so fun to take this photo (page 57); we laughed and kissed a lot. Doesn't this remind you of a Hallmark movie cover? In our house, we have seen just about every Christmas movie and there's always mistletoe involved. Make these cookies and take a super cute photo like this for your Christmas card. Involve the kids by having them pose with their eyes covered! Then you all get cookies to eat!

I used a skinny Christmas tree shape and turned it upside down to make it into mistletoe. This one is so simple and adorable. You will need two shades of green for this cookie, light and dark, to make it look like mistletoe.

From the Kitchen
Skinny Christmas tree-shaped cookies
Batch of buttercream

From the Drawer
White nonpareils or sugar pearls
Tips 4 and 104
Brown, red, and green food coloring gel

Mistletoe Instructions

1. Start piping with your light green and the 104 tip attached. The wide side of the tip should be facing away from you to ¼ inch off your cookie. Squeeze until the buttercream billows out, and pull down and stop squeezing where you want your leaf to end. Sporadically place the same leaves through the tree; this is the bottom layer.

2. With the darker green, pipe a second layer of leaves to fill in the cookie.

3. Pipe some leaves upside down so the mistletoe looks full.

4. Add your white nonpareils or sugar pearls in a cluster of the mistletoe.

5. With brown and tip 4, pipe a thin, straight branch from the base of the leaves to the tip of the cookie.

6. To make this festive and sweet, use red buttercream and tip 4 to make a skinny bow. Start in the center of where you want your bow to be and make two oval loops that both come back to the center. Add two little ribbon tails under that.

MASTER TIP

The skinnier the tree cookie cutter, the more the cookie will resemble mistletoe. Alternating the light green with the dark green gives the cookie some dimension and makes it look accurate. Larger white sugar pearls would also work beautifully.

New Year's Eve
page 68

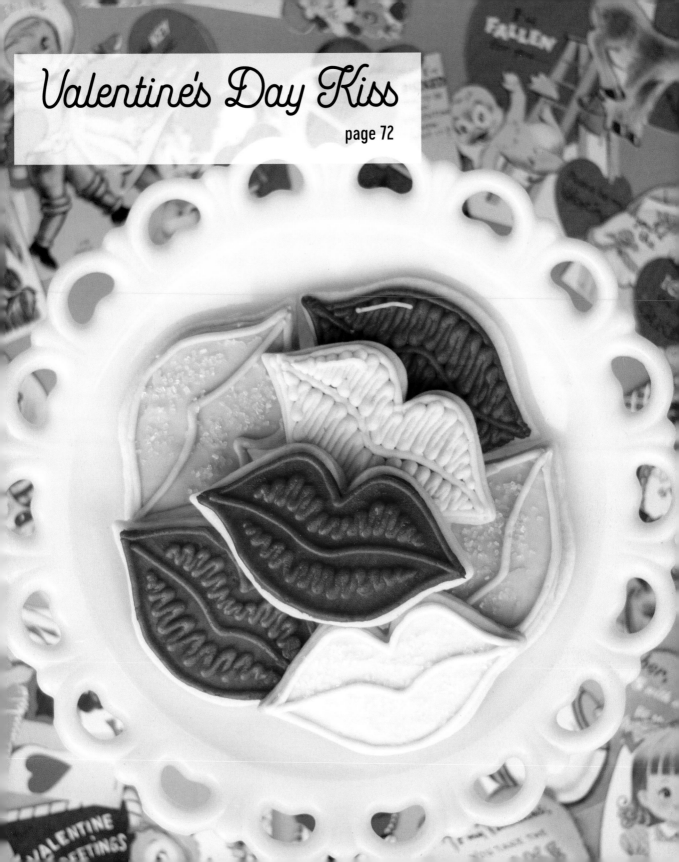

Valentine's Day Kiss

page 72

NEW YEAR'S EVE

New Year's Eve is a fun time to celebrate because we are saying goodbye to the old year and hello to a new year full of possibilities. I like to write out my goals for the new year and reflect on all the events and opportunities from previous years. It's always good to see where we're going, but we can't forget where we've been.

From the Kitchen
Party hat-, champagne glass-, and
   round-shaped cookies
Batch of buttercream
Cup of hot water

From the Drawer
Angled spatula
Tips 12, 4, 5, 21, and 2
Edible gold glitter
Gold and white sugar pearls
Clear sugar crystals
Black, white, pink, yellow, and brown food
   coloring

Clock Instructions

1. Outline and fill the cookie with tip 12 in white buttercream, but don't frost to the very edge because we will be adding a border.

2. Smooth cookie using my smooth buttercream technique on page 3.

3. Add edible glitter to the clock (optional).

4. With black buttercream and tip 5, outline the outside of the clock.

5. Attach tip 2 and pipe the number 12 at the top of the clock. Directly under the 12, add the 6. Go to the right of the cookie to add the 3, and then on the left-hand side add the 9. I piped my clock this way, so my numbers would be evenly placed on the clock. Fill in the rest of the numbers to complete the clock.

6. Make a dot in the middle and a line straight up to the 12 so the clock can read midnight. Make a tiny arrow at the tip. Make another tiny arrow directly under that so both the large hand and the small hand are pointing up.

Pink Champagne on page 70
Party Hat on page 70

Pink Champagne Instructions

1. Outline your cookie with white buttercream and tip 5, but be sure not to pipe to the very edge; you want to be able to turn your cookie without smudging the buttercream.

2. Fill in the champagne glass with either pink or pale brown using tip 5. Pipe back and forth horizontally until the cookie is filled. Leave a tiny space at the top so it looks like the glass isn't filled all the way.

3. Add gold and white sugar pearls to act like the tiny bubbles in the champagne.

MASTER TIPS

To get a champagne color, add a tiny bit of brown to your buttercream and it will be a light tan or champagne color. Mix and match the colors of the party hat to fit any theme.

Party Hat Instructions

1. Start this cookie with tip 5 and black buttercream. Outline your cookie but don't pipe to the very edge; you want to be able to turn your cookie.

2. Separate the hat into three sections to add color.

3. Use yellow buttercream and tip 4 to pipe, and fill in the top and bottom sections of the hat. Pipe in a steady back and forth motion as you fill.

4. For the middle of the hat, use pink buttercream and fill in the middle with tip 4.

5. Next, you need white buttercream and star tip 21. Pipe the top of the hat by squeezing the buttercream out while holding your bag straight up and down about ⅛ inch away from the cookie. Follow the same instructions for piping the white fluffy border of the hat.

6. Add sugar crystals to the finished hat, if desired.

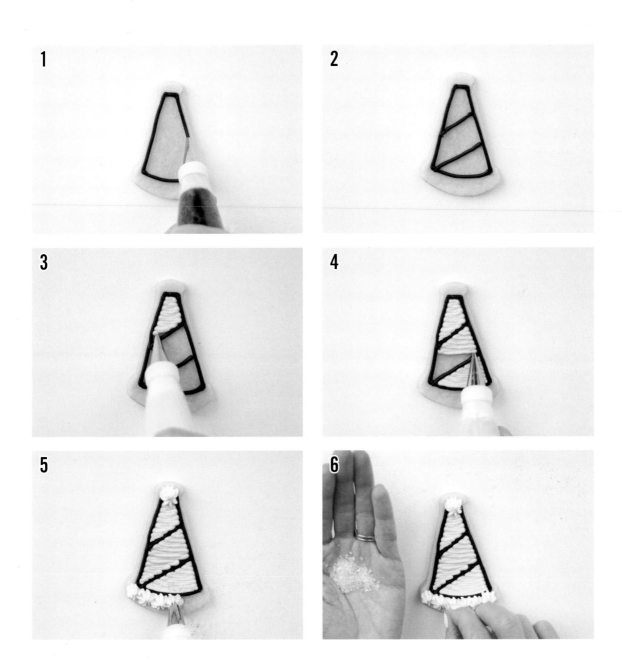

VALENTINE'S DAY KISS

Valentine's Day is easily one of my favorite holidays to decorate and bake for. I love every-thing red and pink. It's a holiday of love so it inspired these lip cookies. Add some edible glitter for extra bling on these luscious smooches. Everyone will be so smitten with the butter-cream lips that they might just lose their fo-kiss.

These cookies would be brilliant for a beauty line with the buttercream matching the lip shade colors they offer. Use them to celebrate the launch of a new color.

From the Kitchen	**From the Drawer**
Lip-shaped cookies	Angled spatula with tapered edge
Batch of buttercream	Clear sugar crystals
Cup of hot water	Tips 2 and 5
	Red, white, and pink food coloring

Smooth Lips Instructions

1. Using red and tip 5, outline your lip cookie but don't pipe to the very edge.

2. Fill in your cookie with a back and forth horizontal motion using the same pressure throughout.

3. With your angled spatula, use my smooth buttercream technique on page 3.

4. After your cookie is nice and smooth, outline the lips with a border.

5. Then draw down the center to give the cookie a top lip and bottom lip.

6. On both the top and bottom, pipe up and down in short squiggly motions to make the creases in the lips.

Textured Lips page 74

Textured Lips Instructions

1. Outline the cookie with tip 5 and pink buttercream. Don't pipe to the very edge; leave a little room to be able to turn the cookie with your hand.

2. Using tip 5, fill in the cookie while piping back and forth horizontally. Angle your piping bag at 45 degrees toward you so the buttercream flows out like a tube of toothpaste.

3. Keep the same pressure throughout the cookie.

4. Pipe down the center to separate the cookie into a top lip and a bottom lip.

5. Use tip 2 with white buttercream and pipe a small, thin line at the top and bottom to make the lip look glossy.

6. Completed cookie.

MASTER TIPS

You can change up the colors and/or not add the squiggly lip creases and add sugar crystals. The possibilities are endless with these. Make ombre lips as a cookie set.

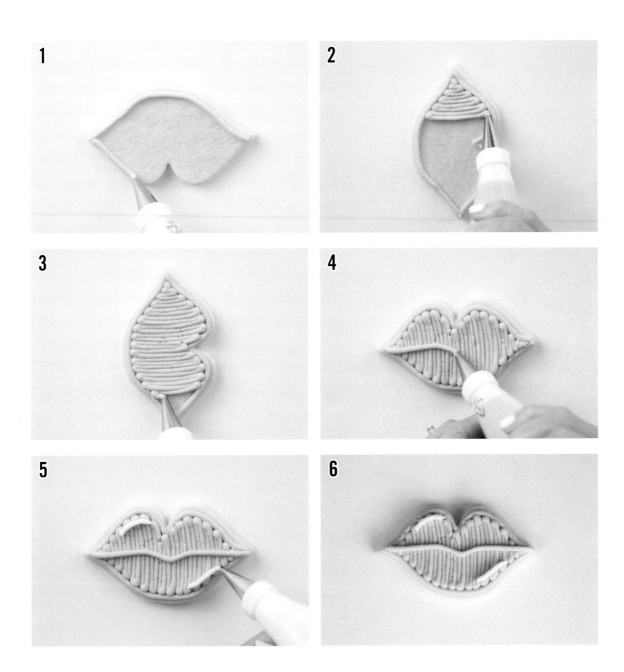

VALENTINE'S DAY FLOWER GARDENS

These gardens are near and dear to my heart; they were specifically created for a television segment I did on Valentine's Day with my friends at Q13Fox in Seattle. The gardens can be used on round or square cookies. My garden cookies are the ones helped launch me into the spotlight. I made round flower gardens with blush pink and light green that landed me on Hallmark's Home and Family for the first time. They quickly became very popular and beloved.

From the Kitchen	From the Drawer
Scalloped heart-shaped cookies	Tips 104, 363, and 18
Batch of buttercream	Dusty rose, green, and red food coloring

Rosette Heart Instructions

1. Using tip 18 and any shade of pink buttercream that matches your garden, start to pipe the rosettes. Start in one corner at the top. Hold your piping bag straight up and down about ⅛ of an inch away from your cookie. Squeeze buttercream and, in one motion, pipe straight down, go around in a circle clockwise, and stop when you get back to the bottom.

2. This should be one easy motion to pipe these mini rosettes. Start to fill in your cookie from top to bottom. The rosettes will fill the cookie and come to a point at the bottom.

Garden on page 78

Garden Instructions

1. Using dusty rose buttercream and tip 104, start in the upper right corner and pipe a peony. The wide end will be at your cookie and the skinny end will be facing away from you. Make a small flat strip and slowly overlap the petals.

2. These petals will be short and overlapped to create the center of the peony. Keep overlapping each petal in sort of an octagon shape for the middle.

3. Turn your cookie as you pipe, the bigger the flower gets, the longer the petals will become. Start to round the shape of the flower. Work outward until the flower is at the desired size.

4. Next, add lilacs. These will be a darker shade of blush by adding a little red food coloring. Using tip 104, face the wide end up this time. Start by squeezing the buttercream out until it billows out the sides and slowly pull back and then stop. Your petals will end when you stop squeezing.

5. Stagger the petals down the cookie, almost bordering the peony. Add one over the other and continue down.

6. To bring the cookie together, add greenery with tip 363 and light green buttercream. Make a cluster by gently squeezing and lifting up so they come to a point.

MASTER TIP

Use different colors for different themes like a wedding, baby shower, or Easter flower gardens. If there are spaces between the flowers, always add more greenery or perhaps little green leaves with a 352 tip.

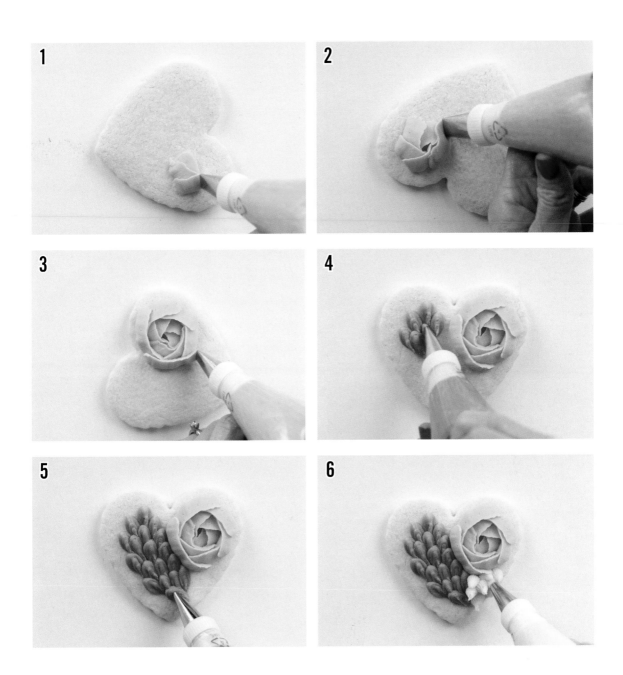

Spring

Flowers come up and the rain goes away, well . . . for the most part. We live in the Pacific Northwest, so we get lots of rain, but the sun starts to peek out in March and that means flowers will start to bloom.

Every year, as a family we go to the tulip fields north of where we live, and there are waves of color as far as the eye can see. It's magical and the perfect spot to stop and take pictures while the sun is setting.

St. Patrick's Day

page 84

Tulip Field

page 88

ST. PATRICK'S DAY

I know St. Patrick's Day is technically in winter, but it feels like it belongs in the spring chapter. Plus, these cookies are so fun—so today is your lucky day. I made little pots of gold, rainbows, shamrocks, and four-leaf clovers. The pots of gold are a fun one that the kids really enjoy—maybe you will catch a Leprechaun with them. Or leave out a plate of these cookies for the Leprechaun to eat and leave real gold coins in their place, hint hint. I'm a lover of traditions and starting new ones to make memories.

From the Kitchen	From the Drawer
Rainbow-, clover- or shamrock-, and round-shaped cookies Batch of buttercream	Gold cake sequins or edible confetti Tips 10, 4, and 125 Black, red, orange, yellow, green, blue, and purple food coloring

Rainbow Instructions

1. Use tip 4 and red buttercream. Pipe to border the top of the rainbow. Draw in short back and forth motions.

2. Use orange buttercream next and create the same pattern.

3. Follow the rainbow colors with yellow buttercream next.

4. Pipe the green buttercream next. Each new color should be piped beneath the previous one.

5. Blue buttercream follows the green.

6. Finish with purple.

Pot O' Gold on page 86
Shamrock or Lucky Clover on page 86

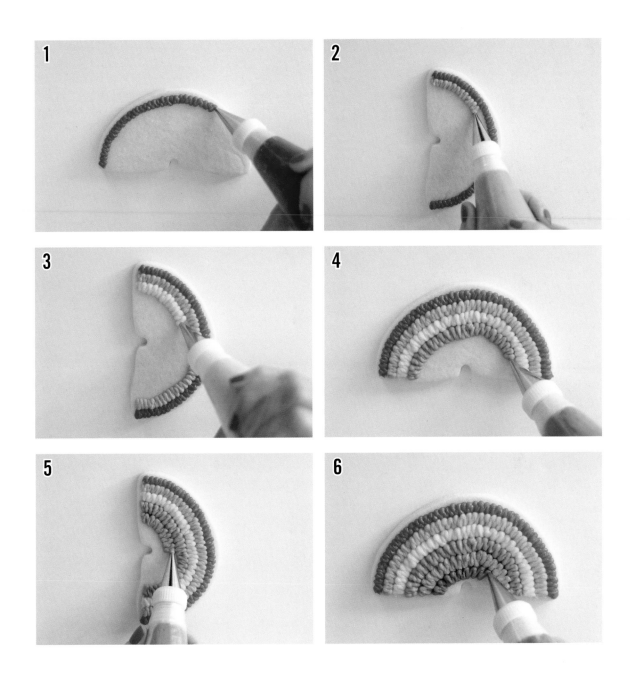

Pot o' Gold instructions

1. Outline with tip 10 and black buttercream, and don't pipe to the very edge—leave room to turn your cookie.

2. Fill in cookie with bright yellow buttercream and tip 10.

3. Finish the cookie with gold cake sequins to look like leprechaun's gold.

MASTER TIP

Tip 5 will also work for rainbow. Another rainbow option would be to draw the buttercream in a straight even line for the rainbow, with each color. I used a vintage spade cookie cutter for the shamrock.

Shamrock or Lucky Clover Instructions

1. Use tip 125 and green buttercream. Have the wide side of the tip facing the edge of the cookie. Pipe until the buttercream puffs out and slowly pull back to create the stem.

2. To make the clover petals, face the skinny side away from you. Pipe in a rounding motion with your wrist to make the petals round as you pipe back down.

3. Create four petals.

4. **For the shamrock**, you will do the same thing with the stem.

5. Point the skinny side toward the edge of the cookie and start piping the shamrock. This time, instead of rounding the petals, you will make one little petal, making a heart shape with the buttercream to create each petal.

6. The motion is small but continue to do that for each petal until you have made three.

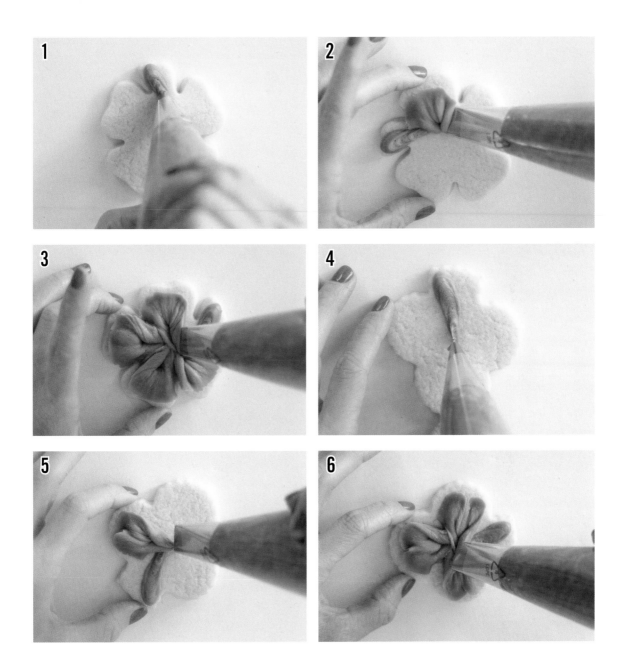

TULIP FIELD

From the Kitchen	From the Drawer
Tulip-shaped cookies	Tips 123 and 104
Batch of buttercream	Green, red, and white food coloring

Instructions

1. Use tip 123 and preferred color of buttercream. Have the skinny end of the tip facing away from you and the wide side facing toward you and almost touching the base of the cookie. Your bag should be at a 45-degree angle. Start in the middle for the first petal and pipe up.

2. Round the top of the petal, and pipe down to create the first petal.

3. From the bottom of the first petal, create the second one to overlap at the base. Pipe up and around and to the right.

4. For the third petal, do the same thing but to the left and bring the petal over the center on the way down.

5. For the green stem, use tip 104 with the wide side of the tip facing the edge. Make the stem by squeezing the buttercream until it billows out and slowly pull back.

6. Make your first leaf with the skinny side facing away from you and the wide side at the base of the cookie. Start to pipe the leaf up half of the tulip.

7. Round at the top and come back down, squeezing an even amount of buttercream.

8. Do the same thing to the other side of the flower.

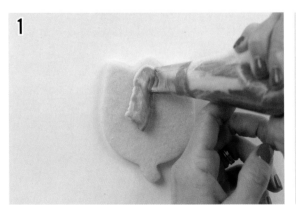

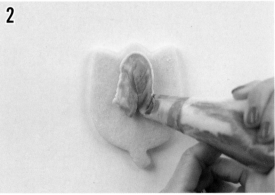

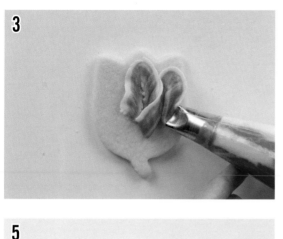

Luke 24: 2-3 *They found the stone rolled away from the tomb, but when they entered, they did not find the body of the Lord Jesus.*

EASTER

Egg hunts, Easter baskets, church service, and brunch are some of my fondest memories. Baskets full of candy is what my kids are excited about. My favorite Easter candy has to be the mini Cadbury eggs. You can usually find them nestled in buttercream on top of my sugar cookies this time of year. Are you excited yet? Well I have more good news: these tutorials are easy and kid-friendly.

From the Kitchen
Egg-, bunny-, chick-, and round-shaped cookies
Batch of buttercream
Cup of hot water

From the Drawer
Angled spatula
Shredded sweetened coconut
Confetti sprinkles
Mini Cadbury chocolate eggs
Tips 233, 47, 5, 10, and 18
Green, pink, yellow, and brown food coloring

Easter Basket Instructions

1. Using brown buttercream and tip 5, outline the bottom half of the basket on the fat part of the egg-shaped cookie. For the top half, make small X's but overlap so it looks like a braided handle.

2. Next, attach tip 47 to make the basket weave, leave a little bit of room between the border and your first vertical strip. Next, horizontally pipe ½-inch strips over top.

3. Leave a ¼-inch space and pipe a second horizontal ½-inch strip. Leave a little more space and draw your second vertical strip. It will start to look like a basket weave.

4. Continue the pattern until the basket is full. Make tiny strips to fill in any empty space.

5. Pipe white buttercream with tip 10 so you can add sprinkles and grass.

6. Add green shredded coconut to the basket (see page 6 for coloring coconut). Finish with confetti sprinkles.

Egg Nest on page 94
Chick on page 94
Bunny on page 95

Egg Nest Instructions

1. Use brown and tip 233 and start piping from the center to the outside of the cookie clockwise and slowly move to the edge of the cookie in a spiral.

2. Make a couple layers with the buttercream to build up the edge of the nest.

3. Add three mini Cadbury eggs to the nests.

Chick Instructions

1. Use yellow buttercream and tip 5 to outline the chick. Fill in the cookie starting at the top by piping horizontally back and forth all the way down.

2. Use my smooth buttercream technique on page 3.

3. Outline the chick.

Bunny Instructions

1. Outline bunny with tip 5 and pink buttercream.
2. Fill in the bunny horizontally.
3. Use my smooth buttercream technique on page 3.
4. Outline the bunny.
5. Use tip 18 and white buttercream to make the tail.
6. Completed bunny cookie.

Use my smooth buttercream technique on page 3.

MASTER TIPS

Feel free to make the colored grass different colors in the Easter baskets. You can also add in jelly beans instead of confetti to the baskets.

WOODLAND WONDERS

This cookie set was inspired by my grandmothers' woods, which she called the Okefenokee Woods. The forest lined her backyard and, as a child, these were magical woods. She told my sisters and me so many stories about the fairies and trolls that lived in the Okefenokees. My grandmother's imagination always had us wide-eyed and begging for more.

From the Kitchen

Deer-, mushroom-, and round-shaped
  cookies
Batch of buttercream
Green crushed graham crackers
  (page 7)

From the Drawer

Tips 10, 104, 363, 5, 4, and 2
Red, white, green, purple, brown, and
  black gel food coloring

Mushroom Instructions

1. Outline the mushroom top with tip 5.

2. Fill in by piping horizontally back and forth.

3. Use my smooth buttercream technique on page 3.

4. With white buttercream and tip 10, pipe the base of the mushroom. Tilt your bag at an angle toward your body to make the buttercream come out like a tube of toothpaste. Make 4 lines down the base.

5. Dip the very tip of the base into green graham crackers for the moss.

6. Finish off with large white polka dots. Hold your piping bag straight up and down and squeeze until the buttercream billows out to make the desired size. Stop squeezing and then pull up.

Fawn on page 98
Mossy Flowers on page 99

Fawn Instructions

1. Outline fawn with tip 4 and white buttercream. Don't pipe to the very edge.

2. Fill in while piping back and forth horizontally. Hold the piping bag at a 45-degree angle so it flows like a tube of toothpaste.

3. Use tip 2 and pipe 6 little spots on the rear end in brown buttercream. Color the inside of ears in a short back and forth motion. Pipe a dot for the nose. Next, use black buttercream and make a closed eye, almost like an elongated sideways S.

4. Completed fawn.

MASTER TIPS

Make the flowers different colors. Put different styles of flowers in the center; a lily would be beautiful. The baby fawn could be light brown with white accents, as well.

Mossy Flower Instructions

1. Use green buttercream with tip 10. Pipe two layers on the outside of cookie. Don't pipe to very edge.

2. Dip cookie straight down into green graham crackers. Gently press to coat and pull up.

3. Use tip 104 with purple and white buttercream. For a refresher on making two-toned buttercream, see page 4. Gently pipe with the wide side almost touching the center and the skinny end of the piping tip up. Make a rounding motion with your wrist to make each petal. Keep turning your cookie as you pipe.

4. Use light green to make a center with tip 363.

Summer

One of the things my family and I enjoy about summer is the farmers' markets with fresh produce. I enjoy adding fresh berries to the buttercream to make a tasty treat.

My family and I are outdoorsy people who like to hike together and play the game "Would you rather" as we walk. It's funny to hear what your kids come up with. "Would you rather eat spaghetti or tacos for the rest of your life?" My boys make me laugh so hard with these. You can't have summer without a few epic hikes.

This year, we took our first ever family vacation to Maui (Disneyland doesn't count as vacation, in my opinion). The beautiful golden beaches and fragrant hibiscus flowers inspired some cookies in this chapter.

Summer Fruit Cookies

page 104

Aloha Cookies

page 106

SUMMER FRUIT COOKIES

My family loves picking berries in the summer. Fresh-picked fruit will add an extra-special flavor to your buttercream. I Included lemons, as well as berries, because I love everything lemon.

These cookies were inspired by the memories of my kids picking berries with their stained fingers and faces. How fun would the lemon cookies be at a lemonade stand!

From the Kitchen	From the Drawer
Berry- and lemon-shaped cookies	Angled spatula
Batch of berry or lemon buttercream (page 35)	Sugar crystals
Cup of hot water	Tips 5, 10, 12, and 352
	Green gel food coloring

Lemon Instructions

1. Outline and fill cookie using tip 10 and lemon buttercream.

2. Use smooth buttercream technique on page 3.

3. Outline edge with tip 5. Sprinkle with sugar crystals.

Strawberry Instructions

1. Outline and fill cookie with tip 10 and strawberry buttercream.

2. Use smooth buttercream technique on page 3.

3. Pipe leaves using green buttercream and tip 352. Hold the beak of the tip facing down, as pictured. Stop squeezing where you want the leaf to end.

Raspberry Instructions

1. Use raspberry buttercream and tip 12. Hold piping bag ⅛ inch away from cookie and squeeze until the buttercream billows out. Stop squeezing where you want the dollop to stop and pull up.

2. With green buttercream and tip 352, make small leaves at the top of the berry.

ALOHA COOKIES

These cookies remind me of the beauty of Maui, Hawaii. Our family took a vacation here and enjoyed every second. We swam with turtles, snorkeled with tropical fish, and ate the most delicious food. We laid on the golden beaches, swam in the ocean, and played in the waves. My kids and I noticed that the birds hung out in pairs, as if they had a buddy system. We saw little lizards, mountain goats, and the most gorgeous waterfalls. My family and I really soaked in time together on our trip, and I cried on the way to the airport because Maui truly is magical and has our hearts. These cookies were inspired by our love for the island.

From the Kitchen
Round-, hibiscus-, and palm tree–shaped cookies

From the Drawer
Graham cracker sleeve or 8 crackers
Rolling pin
Angled spatula
Tips 104, 352, 5, 10, and 2
Fuchsia, hot pink, yellow, green, turquoise blue, brown, and white food coloring

Palm Tree Instructions

1. Use tip 104 and brown buttercream. Pipe at the base of tree. Hold the wide end of the tip facing away from you.

2. Pipe and overlap slightly for texture.

3. With green and leaf tip 352, pipe palm leaves by squeezing and slowly dragging to make a long leaf. The beak should be facing down on the tip, as pictured.

4. Make leaves to fill the tree.

5. Finish with small leaves on the center layers.

6. Completed tree.

Hibiscus on page 108
Pineapple Top on page 109
Beach Wave on page 110

Hibiscus Instructions

1. Fill a bag with two-toned buttercream (page 4) and add tip 104. Point the wide side of the tip toward the cookie and skinny side up, like pictured. Pipe first petal at a 45-degree angle and round the tip as you come back inward.
2. Create each petal by squeezing with the same pressure.
3. Turn your cookie as you go, creating 5 petals total.
4. With tip 10 and white buttercream, start in the middle and angle piping bag for tube of toothpaste–like flow to create the flowers pistil.
5. Make tiny dots on end with tip 2.
6. Completed flower.

Pineapple Top Instructions

1. Use yellow buttercream and tip 104 to pipe pineapple top. Pipe on the outside but not on the very edge. The tip's wide end should face away from you

2. Go all the way around the cookie in a circle.

3. Create the second layer by overlapping the first layer.

4. The final layer will be small bursts of buttercream to cover the top.

5. With green buttercream and tip 352, pipe on the leaves. Hold the beak facing down. Squeeze buttercream until it comes out the sides and pull back and stop piping.

6. For the center leaves, pipe and pull upward.

Beach Wave Instructions

1. With light turquoise buttercream and tip 5, outline waves and fill in.

2. Use an angled spatula to smooth out buttercream. Don't use my smooth buttercream technique here; it looks natural when just gently smoothed.

3. With a darker shade and tip 5, pipe onto waves.

4. Smooth that out, as well.

5. Pipe on a second layer of waves.

6. Repeat with darker blue and smooth once again.

7. Crush graham crackers with rolling pin (see technique on page 7). Sprinkle the cracker crumbs on the edge of the water to create sandy beach edge.

8. Finished beach cookie.

MASTER TIPS

Make hibiscus flower any bright colors. Add coconuts to the palm tree using tip 5 and brown buttercream.

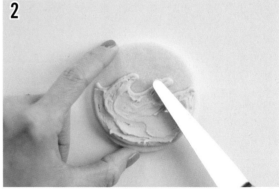

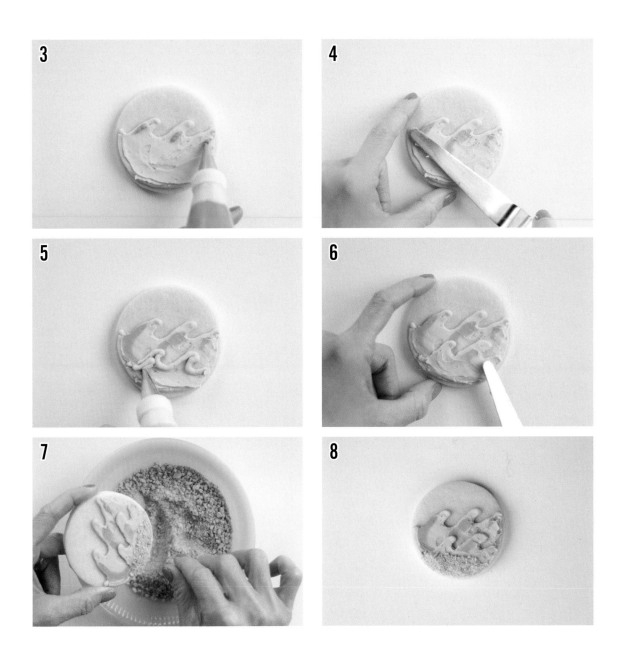

Terrarium Succulent Cookies

page 114

Fourth of July

page 120

TERRARIUM SUCCULENT COOKIES

Aloe there, I hope you like these cookies because they definitely don't succ. Ha, I amuse myself so much sometimes, but let me get to the point . . . this plate of cookies is looking sharp.

I love succulents and terrariums so I thought we could make them with a marbled glaze base. Make sure to let your glaze dry overnight before piping on them. You can make them without the glaze as well.

From the Kitchen	From the Drawer
Marbled honey glaze (page 36)	Tips 352, 103, 104, 363, 4, and 18
Diamond- and round-shaped cookies	Green and pink food coloring
Batch of buttercream	

Prickly Succulent Instructions

1. Use green buttercream and tip 352. Hold the beak facing down and angled at 45-degrees toward you. Pipe until the buttercream billows out and slightly pull back to make first leaf.

2. Pipe all the way around but don't pipe on very edge.

3. Make a second layer.

4. Continue to pipe and fill the plant until it's complete.

5. Pipe the center leaves up rather than out.

6. Completed cookie.

Leafy Succulent on page 116
Terrarium on page 118

Leafy Succulent Instructions

1. Use tip 104 and pale green buttercream. You can also use a two-toned buttercream like I did here (instructions on page 4). Hold the wide side of tip against the cookie; the skinny end should face up. Hold piping bag at a 45-degree angle.

2. Keep piping these leaves as you turn your cookie. Don't pipe to the very edge.

3. For second layer, pipe smaller leaves.

4. For these leaves, don't round your wrist. Pipe with good pressure, and when it gets to the tip, slow down and come back inward.

5. Make very small leaves for the top layer.

6. Completed cookie.

MASTER TIP

Use two-toned buttercream for realistic succulents. Pink (like I used for the Leafy Succulent), turquoise, or purple work great with the green. Take unglazed cookies and spray them with edible gold spray and then pipe on the terrarium and succulents. Find the spray online or at a craft store where they sell baking supplies. Make pale green buttercream with a tiny bit of green so it is very light.

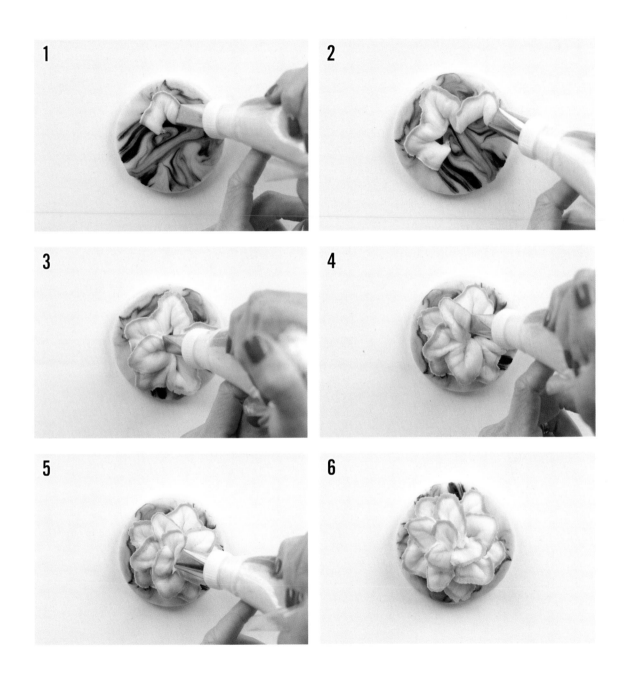

Terrarium Instructions

1. Outline diamond-shaped cookie with tip 4 and white buttercream.
2. Make two small lines up from the bottom.
3. Connect with a horizontal line.
4. Pipe two lines up to the tip.
5. Make small leafy succulent with tip 103 in one corner.
6. Make dark green prickly succulent in the other corner following tutorial on page 116.
7. With light green and tip 363, hold the bag straight up and down and pipe dollops of buttercream for the small cacti. Fill in open spots on the terrarium.
8. Finish with star tip 18 and pink buttercream. Make small flowers on cacti.

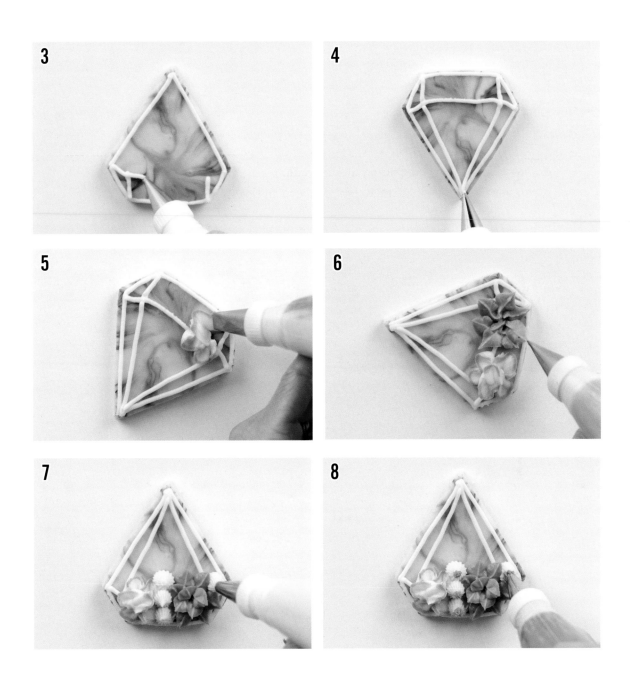

FOURTH OF JULY

Every year on the Fourth of July, my family has a much-anticipated reunion. This get-together has all the bells and whistles. We play games, eat delicious food, and light up the sky with fireworks. This plate is inspired by the fun memories we make every year.

From the Kitchen
Watermelon-, popsicle-, round-, and
  number 4-shaped cookies
Batch of buttercream
Cup of hot water

From the Drawer
Angled spatula
Tweezers
Sugar crystals
Star sprinkles
Tips 12, 5, 18, 5, and 2
Red, white, blue, pink, green, and black
  food coloring

Flag Instructions

1. With tip 18 and blue, start with a rosette at the top, off-centered. Pipe a rosette by holding your bag at a 45-degree angle. Pipe down, around clockwise, and back to the bottom and stop.

2. Right next to the blue, pipe a red buttercream rosette with tip 18. Then for the second row, all the way to the left, pipe second and third blue rosettes.

3. Pipe a row of two white rosettes. There will be a total of four in this row, including the blue.

4. The third row of blue will have three rosettes. Make three red rosettes next to the blue. A row of six white rosettes will go under that. Make a shorter row of four red rosettes.

5. Finish with two white rosettes at the bottom.

6. Use tweezers to place white stars on the flag.

Watermelon on page 122
4th on page 124
Popsicle on page 124

Watermelon Instructions

1. Outline watermelon with pink buttercream and tip 5. Leave room for the rind.

2. Fill in horizontally back and forth with piping bag at an angle for tube of toothpaste-like flow.

3. Pipe first layer of rind with white buttercream and tip 5.

4. Pipe lighter green buttercream against white with tip 5.

5. Pipe darker green with tip 2 for outside.

6. Use black buttercream and tip 2 to pipe seeds. Pipe a small dot and slowly move back as you stop squeezing to get the seed shape.

MASTER TIPS

You can make the watermelon cookie red instead of pink—and you can use my smooth buttercream technique on this cookie, as well. Make the popsicle all different colors. The 4 can be made into different numbers and colors to celebrate birthdays or anniversaries.

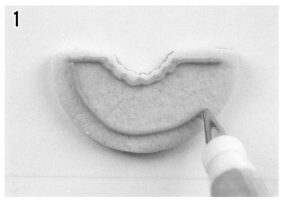

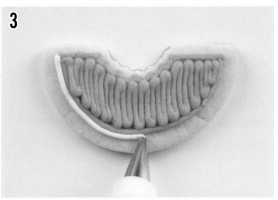

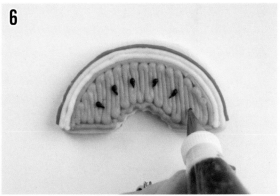

4th Cookie Instructions

1. Use tip 12 to pipe red, white, and blue dollops of buttercream.
2. Continue until 4 is full alternating red, white, and blue.

Popsicle Instructions

1. Use tip 12 with white buttercream to outline and fill popsicle but leave stick unfrosted.
2. Use my smooth buttercream technique on page 3.
3. Make a dab of red and blue buttercream on the popsicle.
4. Smooth again. Then sprinkle with clear sugar crystals.
5. Outline popsicle with tip 5.
6. Use tip 12 to pipe light brown for the stick.

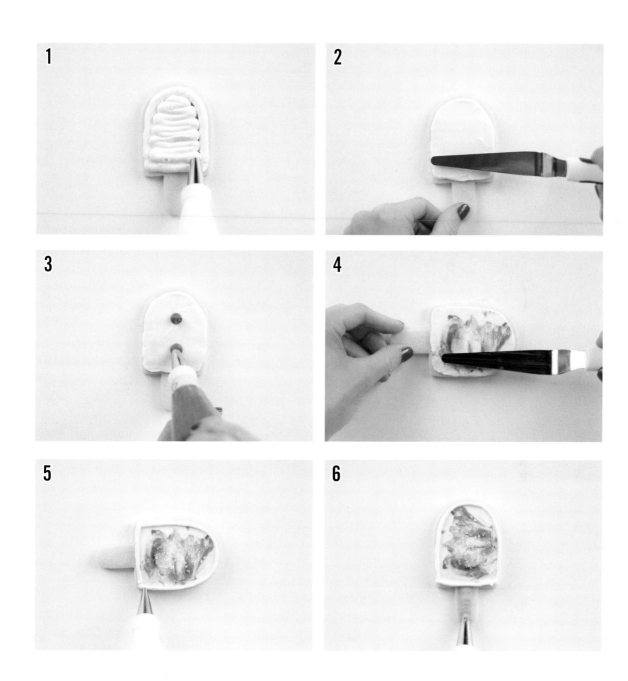

Very truly I tell you, you will weep and mourn while the world rejoices, you will grieve, but your grief will turn to joy. John 16:20

Fall

The nights get longer, the air gets colder, and pumpkin spice is in everything. I love fall for so many reasons, but the main one is that it means the holidays aren't far away.

My family and I have fun dressing up and decorating for Halloween. Some of my fondest memories are thinking back to all the costumes we've worn over the years. It's especially fun when your kids love dressing up, too. My son Mikie went through a Batman stage where he had to be Batman every year for five years.

Our Jenny's birthday is on Halloween, so we go to the cemetery and bring her a specially carved pumpkin to light by her grave. It's important to us to keep her memory alive. We pray over her headstone, thank God for everything He has done, and love on each other because we all miss her.

Pumpkin Tops

page 130

Witchy Halloween

page 132

PUMPKIN TOPS

My pumpkin top cookies are my most innovative cookies and the ones I'm most proud of. I loved seeing everyone's version of this cookie as it quickly spread on the Internet. These little pumpkin tops are just so adorable and make me happy. This cookie sparked the aerial view that I keep repeating though the book. I love getting a different view on the norm.

From the Kitchen	From the Drawer
Circle cookies	Tips 125, 21, and 2
Batch of buttercream	Orange, brown, and green

Instructions

1. Start piping your pumpkin on a circle cookie with the wide side of your tip facing the outside of the cookie.

2. Don't pipe to the very edge—leave room to turn your cookie without messing up the buttercream.

3. Squeeze until you see the buttercream billow out and slowly pull to the center of the cookie and stop. Repeat all the way around the cookie.

4. I normally pipe 10 to 12 sections depending on the size of my cookie.

5. Using the brown and tip 21, pipe your stem in the center of the cookie. Start squeezing and pull up.

6. Stop squeezing when you want your stem to end. Add three vines with tip 2 on the top of the pumpkin with your green buttercream.

MASTER TIP

I love to use white or light green to make Cinderella pumpkins. Try to avoid stacking directly on top of the stem to avoid crushing. Remember the buttercream crusts over; it doesn't get hard.

WITCHY HALLOWEEN

These cookies remind me of my daughter Reese when she was just a little girl. Every year she wanted to be a cute little witch. She chose a different color costume each year, purple being my favorite. Her sweet costume inspired these Halloween cookies. Reese also loved glitter, so I added edible glitter onto the witch hats. Black sugar crystals would also make a pretty touch and add a little sparkle to the witch hats. My kids love the part when they get to add sugar crystals or sprinkles.

Adding little brooms would be super cute and bring some "Hocus Pocus" to the cookies.

From the Kitchen

Witch hat-, cat face-, and round-shaped cookies
Batch of buttercream
Cup of hot water

From the Drawer

Tips 12, 102, and 5
Angled spatula
Candy eyes
Halloween sprinkles
Black, purple, and neon green food coloring

Witch Hat Instructions

1. Outline the hat with tip 5 in black buttercream.

2. Draw three lines down the hat to separate into smaller sections.

3. Starting at the top, squeeze with a stronger amount of pressure, and move down slowly. This acts as a fill method for decorating these cookies. Repeat until you are finished.

4. Next you need the purple with tip 102 for the witch's ribbon. You'll want the wide side against the black already piped, and the skinny side facing toward the brim of the hat.

5. Attach tip 12 to the black buttercream and pipe on the brim of the hat. You will want to hold your piping bag straight up and down and about ⅛ of a distance from the cookie to create a flatter look.

6. Optional: add edible black glitter.

Witch Cauldron on page 134
Black Cat on page 134

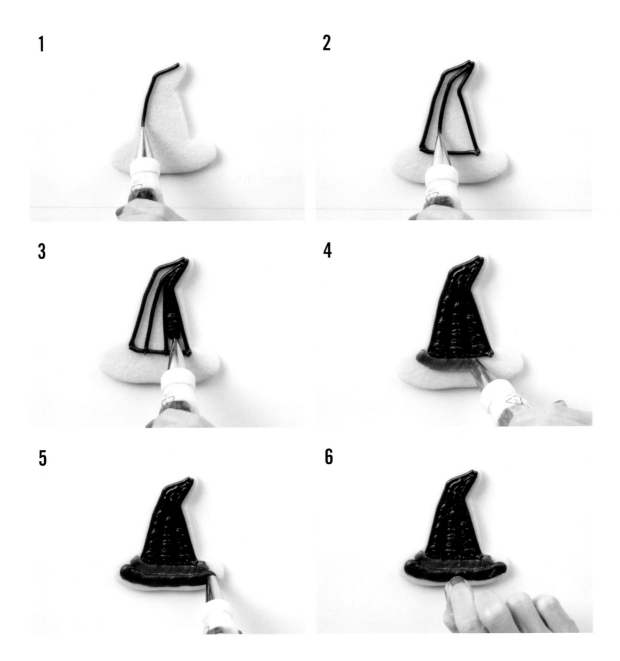

Witch Cauldron Instructions

1. Start with black buttercream and tip 12 to make a circle around the cookie. If you tilt your piping bag, the buttercream will come out in a tube.

2. Use tip 12 and neon green buttercream to make the witches' brew. Go over the black rim a little to make it look like the witches' brew is bubbling out. Make the green wavy to look bubbly as you fill in the center.

3. Add in candy bones, candy eyes, and Halloween-themed confetti sprinkles to complete cauldron.

Black Cat Instructions

1. Use tip 12 with the black buttercream as you outline and fill your cookie.

2. Use my smooth buttercream technique from page 3.

3. Attach tip 5 to the black and add tiny ears by outlining and filling in.

4. Add a little nose and mouth.

5. Add candy eyes.

6. Completed black cat.

MASTER TIP

You can use chocolate buttercream and color with black to prevent having to add a ton of food coloring gel. I add a little yellow food coloring to my green to get a neon green color.

Pumpkin Pie Slice

page 138

Cherry and Pumpkin Cookie Pies

page 140

PUMPKIN PIE SLICE

What does a pumpkin pie say after a big meal? That was filling. Ha, silly joke, I know, but pumpkin pie is a family favorite so I couldn't resist. The very first thing I can remember baking with my grandma as a child is pumpkin pie. It brings back so many fond memories in the kitchen. What better way to make some memories of your own than with these pumpkin pie slices?

These little slices have a special touch of pumpkin pie seasoning on top that also adds a festive flavor to the buttercream.

From the Kitchen
Triangle cookies
Pumpkin pie spice
Batch of buttercream

From the Drawer
Tips 5, 12, and 21
Orange, light brown, and white food coloring

Instructions

1. Outline your triangle cookie with tip 5 and don't pipe to the very edge. Leave room at the top where your crust will go.

2. Hold your piping bag at a 45-degree angle and pipe back and forth horizontally, all the way down the cookie until it fills the pie slice.

3. Turn the cookie around and with tip 12, pipe the crust using light brown at a slightly tilted angle with a steady flow.

4. Sprinkle with pumpkin pie spice.

5. For the last step, add your white whipped cream with tip 21 to finish off this darling cookie. To get the perfect dollop, I hold my piping tip close to the cookie and keep squeezing while slowly pulling up and then stop with your piping bag straight up and down.

6. Completed cookie.

MASTER TIP

To practice the whip cream dollop, use a plate to see how the star tip works best for you. You can add ¼ to ½ teaspoons of pumpkin pie spice directly into your batch of buttercream before you color it orange if you want it to taste festive. Coloring buttercream can be tricky; I use a little brown in my orange for a true pumpkin pie color.

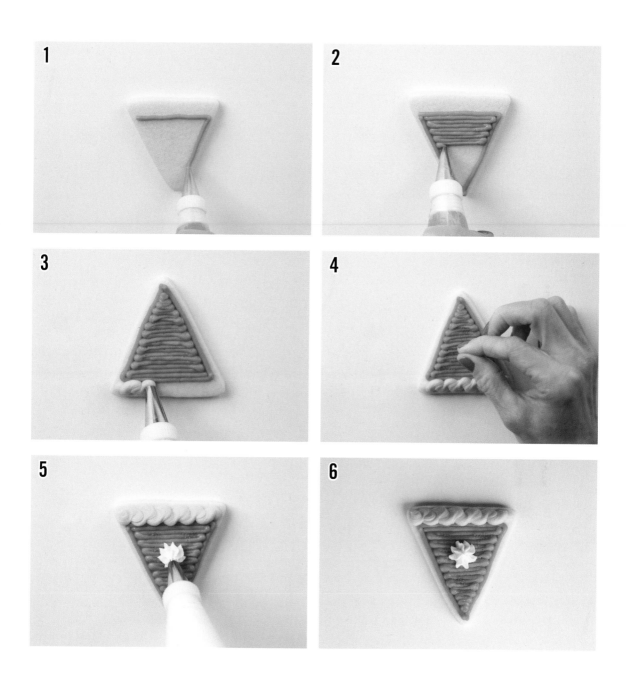

CHERRY AND PUMPKIN COOKIE PIES

Fall brings us into Thanksgiving, and the first thing besides my family that comes to mind is pie! We love a good pie in our house so I was inspired to make these pie cookies. Did you catch that?!! I said PIE COOKIES. This cookie is one of my most innovative cookies. I created this for Thanksgiving one year and people went crazy for them. I could also picture this look on the top of a cupcake. This is one of my designs that can be used on more than cookies, even on a larger scale to top a cake.

From the Kitchen
Large round cookies (about 4 inches)
Pie crust
Egg for egg wash
Slightly smaller round cookie cutter for
  the crust (3 inches)
Cherry pie filling
Pumpkin pie spice
Batch of buttercream

From the Drawer
Rolling pin
Pastry cutter
Pastry brush
Parchment paper
Cupcake tin
Nonstick spray
Angled spatula
Tips 12, 10, and 21
Orange, light brown, and white food
  coloring

Cherry Pie Crust Instructions

1. Preheat oven to 450°F. I used a premade pie crust for the topper, but you can make your own from scratch. Lay flat and rolled out. Use a ruler to measure each strip to ¼-inch width and cut into strips using a pizza cutter, pastry cutter, or a knife.

2. Use the lattice technique for the pie crust. This will take a little time because the strips are so small. Make the lattice tight.

3. Pull up every other strip and lay one horizontally. Lay over the ones you pulled up. Pull up the opposite strips and lay another one down horizontally. Repeat these steps.

4. Once this is completed, brush with a tiny bit of water or egg wash to make the crust stick together.

5. Place a piece of parchment paper over crust and gently roll the top to bind the crust together. Do not make flat.

6. Use the 3-inch cookie cutter to cut out the pie tops.

Cherry Pie Crust continued on page 142
Assemble Cherry Pie Filling on page 142
Pumpkin Pie on page 144

...Cherry Pie Continued

7. Flip over cupcake tin, spray with nonstick spray, add pie crusts on tin, and sprinkle with sugar.

8. Bake at 450°F for 5 to 7 minutes. Keep an eye on them.

9. Remove from oven and let cool.

Cherry Pie Assembly

1. Grab your large cookie and add a thick border of buttercream for the crust using tip 12. Make it look wavy like a real pie crust.

2. Add a small spoonful of the cherry pie filling to the center of the cookie.

3. Place the pie crust directly on top.

MASTER TIP

I use canned cherry pie filling because it isn't too sweet. I suggest making your own easy pie filling if you want to use apple, strawberry, or raspberry because the canned is just too sweet. A tart jam would work great, as well. You want to balance out the sweetness of the buttercream. The cupcake pan works great for pie crusts because it makes edges round over slightly to make room for the filling.

Pumpkin Pie Instructions

1. Use tip 12 to pipe on your orange for the pumpkin pie but leave some space around the edge for your pie crust.

2. Use my smooth buttercream technique from page 3.

3. Add your pie crust with tip 10.

4. Follow all the way around your cookie and use a wavy motion to make the crust.

5. Sprinkle with pumpkin pie spice.

6. Finish with tip 21 for the whip. Hold your piping bag ⅛ inch off cookie and squeeze until the buttercream billows out the sides and slowly pull up. Stop squeezing where you want the buttercream to stop.

MASTER TIP

Add in ¼ to ½ teaspoon pumpkin pie spice to the orange buttercream when you are mixing your colors to give the cookie a festive taste. I add some brown food coloring into my orange to get the pumpkin pie color of buttercream. Change the buttercream color to yellow for a banana or lemon cream pie and omit the pumpkin pie spice. Brown buttercream works for chocolate cream pie.

THANKSGIVING

These cookies will get gobbled up on the Thanksgiving table. Family time is so important, so I wanted to include cookies that your kids can get involved in making. The marbled leaves are fun for the whole family because they can gently knead the dough with gloves on and see the colors mixing.

The turkey cookie is simple enough, and you can get more detailed on the face if you would like, but I think he is charming the way he is. I do have a serious question: Why can't you take a turkey to church? Because they have fowl language!

From the Kitchen	**From the Drawer**
Pilgrim hat-, 3-inch round-, and leaf-shaped cookies Batch of buttercream	Tips 5, 104, 12, 2, and 10 Red, yellow, orange, brown, and black food coloring

Fall Leaf Instructions

1. Use the marbled cookie method (page 36), but use fall colors.

2. Attach tip 5 to your brown buttercream and pipe the main vein of the leaf. Continue piping until you have created all the veins in the leaf.

Turkey on page 148
Pilgrim hat on page 150

Turkey Instructions

1. Start with your red buttercream. Use tip 104 with the skinny side of the tip facing the edge of the cookie. Gently squeeze while creating a ruffle that goes halfway around your cookie.

2. With orange buttercream, use the same method to make second layer.

3. For your last layer, use yellow and slightly overlap orange but leave room for the body.

4. Make a larger mound for the body with brown buttercream and tip 12. Stop squeezing and pull up for a clean break in the buttercream. Make the turkey head just above the body with brown and tip 12. Squeeze buttercream until desired shape overlaps yellow feathers.

5. Attach tip 2 to the orange and make little feet.

6. Also make your turkey beak with the same tip and color as the feet.

7. With black buttercream and tip 2, add tiny little eyes.

8. Completed turkey.

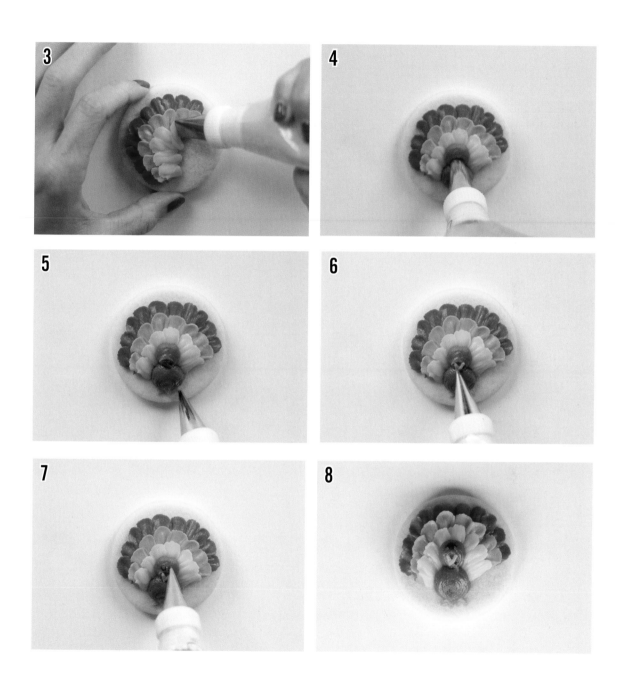

Pilgrim Hat Instructions

1. Start with tip 10 and the black buttercream. Outline the top part of the hat.

2. Make two stripes down the hat to fill it in.

3. Make a stripe of brown buttercream with tip 12, along the bottom of the black to make a leather strip.

4. Attach tip 12 to your black to make a thick brim of the hat. Hold your bag straight up and down about ⅛ inch off your cookie to make it pipe flatter.

5. Using tip 2, pipe a yellow buckle to finish the hat.

6. Finished hat.

MASTER TIP

The longer you squeeze before lifting up the bag while piping the turkey body, the larger your dollop of buttercream will be.

I used a witch hat cookie cutter and cut the tip off before I baked my pilgrim hat cookie.

Add edible glitter to your fall leaf cookie.

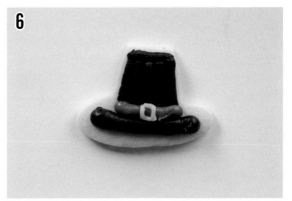

"Bloom where you are planted." —Mother Theresa

Flowers

My favorite chapter in the book is this one! These cookies have been innovated and crafted with love and care.

When I look at a beautiful bouquet of flowers, my first thought is: *How can I turn these into a cookie?* I experience so much joy and excitement when I create buttercream flowers. This chapter is more advanced, but with practice, I have faith that my step-by-step photos and detailed instructions for each flower will help you achieve success with each!

To create my flower gardens, make smaller scales of any design and put them on one cookie.

Bouquet of Pink

page 156

Bowl of Roses

page 160

BOUQUET OF PINK

These flower cookies are near and dear to my heart. Peonies and anemone flowers are my favorite. I love how unique they are and the beauty they add to any bouquet makes them magnificent. The peony was my first flower tutorial I ever created. When decorators were making ruffles and rosette cookies, I wanted to stand out so I made the peony flower cookie, and that blossomed my desire to create all my favorite flowers. It also has inspired so many others to keep creating, and that is so fun to watch.

The anemone needs no explanation; this flower has always stood out and made an impact. I created this one first in pink buttercream and then white.

From the Kitchen
Round cookies
Batch of buttercream

From the Drawer
Tips 2 and 104
Pink, green, fuchsia, white, and black food coloring

Light Pink Peony Instructions

1. Pipe a dollop of green buttercream in the center of the cookie using tip 2.
2. Use a lighter green buttercream and tip 104. Hold the wide end of the tip facing the cookie and the skinny tip facing up. Start piping little strips that overlap and round the center.
3. Pipe all the way around for the center of the flower.
4. Use light pink buttercream and tip 104. Pipe the petals longer as the flower gets bigger.
5. Keep piping around.
6. Work your way to the edge of the cookie.

Fuchsia Peony on page 158
Anemone on page 159

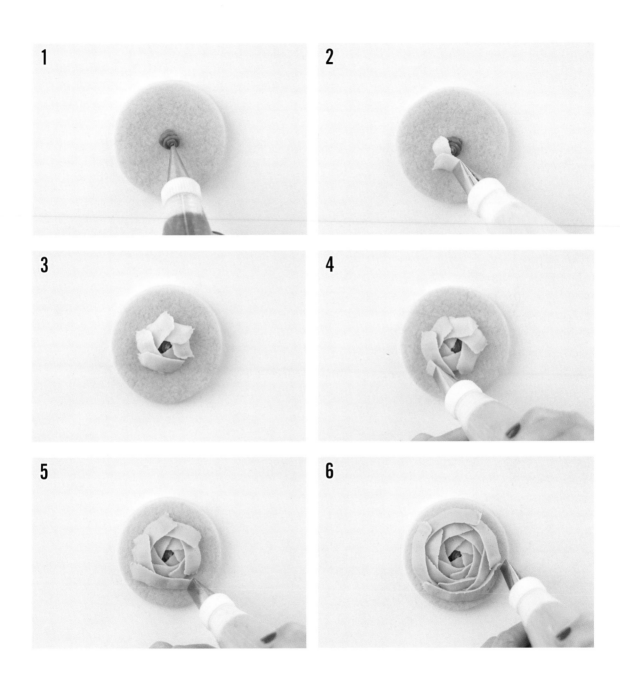

Fuchsia Peony Instructions

1. Use white buttercream to make a dollop in the center with tip 2. Make tiny dots on the top to create center of flower.

2. Use tip 104 and fuchsia buttercream. Hold the wide end facing the cookie and the skinny end facing up, as pictured.

3. Slowly make the petals around the center. There should be five.

4. Make the second layer.

5. As the petals get larger, you will start to angle the tip toward you so the petals open up.

6. Continue to open up the petals until you're at the edge of the cookie.

MASTER TIPS

Some of the prettiest flowers are pink anemones; color buttercream pink or use my two-toned technique on page 4 to add pink in the center of the petals. Change the colors in the centers of the flowers for a different look.

Anemone Instructions

1. Create the first petal with tip 104 and white buttercream. The wide side should face in, touching the cookie, and the skinny end should face away from you. Hold the piping bag at a 45-degree angle. Starting in the center of the cookie, squeeze the buttercream and slowly pipe up, slightly over, and down to create petals.

2. Pipe five petals for the bottom layer.

3. Make a second but smaller layer of petals and round each one with a slight wrist movement as you turn the cookie.

4. Make four top petals and close the flower.

5. With black buttercream and tip 2, make the center of the flower and fill it in.

6. Using the same tip, make tiny dots around the center.

BOWL OF ROSES

This beautiful vintage bowl is full of buttercream roses. These classic roses go perfectly on cookies. Pale buttercream roses pair nicely with chocolate or red velvet cookies. I've loved experimenting over the years with all different color palettes. I am always inspired by nature's beauty; that's why my flowers chapter is my favorite. You will be amazed at how simple these really are to make.

It took a lot of self-control not to call these cookies Rose Bowl and I chuckle at that.

From the Kitchen	From the Drawer
Round cookies	Tip 104
Batch of buttercream	Red food coloring

Instructions

1. Take tip 104 and red buttercream. Have the wide end at the cookie and the skinny end upwards. The piping bag will be at a 45-degree angle towards the cookie. Pipe a little bit of buttercream as the base. On top of that, squeeze and turn the cookie to make a cone for the bud.

2. Make the first layer of petals by piping small strips of buttercream as the petals.

3. I normally make five center petals that slightly overlap each other. Slowly work your way-out creating layers of petals. As the bud gets larger, the petals will get longer.

4. The farther you work your way outside of the cookie, keep tilting your bag at a lower angle to be a flatter surface, as pictured, so the petals have a bit of a lip or curl on them.

5. Continue to make more overlapping petals.

6. Make the last layer of petals long to bring it together and close the flower.

MASTER TIPS

The rose is all about the petals. Make shorter petals for the center and longer to close the flower at the end. The more you angle the tip, the more open your flower will become. For the deep red I use Wilton's no-taste red food coloring gel and color C in the color right system. If you hold the bag at a 0-degree angle perpendicular with the table, you will have open petals. Practice on a paper towel before going to a cookie.

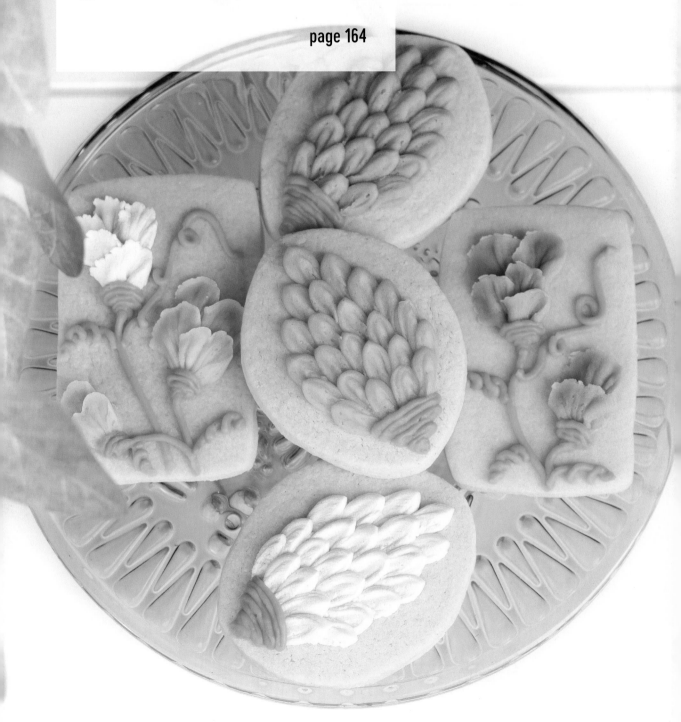

Sweetest Flowers

page 164

Tea Time Flowers

page 168

SWEETEST FLOWERS

I was inspired to make these because they are some of my favorite flowers that just so happen to also be some of the sweetest. I love the magical, whimsical looking vines on the sweet peas. When I first developed the lilac, I made them on square and rectangle cookies and the tutorial I made for them went viral. My lilacs are such a versatile technique that has inspired bakers and decorators because of its wide range of uses. You can even use my technique to decorate bird feathers, mermaid tails, lion's manes, and so many more.

From the Kitchen	From the Drawer
Rectangle- and oval-shaped cookies	Tips 104 and 2
Batch of buttercream	white, pink, purple, and green gel food coloring

Lilac Instructions

1. Use pink or purple buttercream with tip 104. Have the wide end of the tip facing away from you and the skinny end toward you. Start in the top corner of your cookie. Squeeze the buttercream until you see it billow out the sides and slowly pull down for each petal.

2. Work your way down and slightly overlap the petals, getting wider as you go.

3. As you get to the middle, you will slowly start to bring it down to a point.

4. Slightly stagger and overlap the petals.

5. Get skinnier as you reach the bottom of the flower.

6. Complete the lilac with green buttercream and tip 2. Pipe back and forth horizontally to make the base of the stem.

Sweet Pea page 166

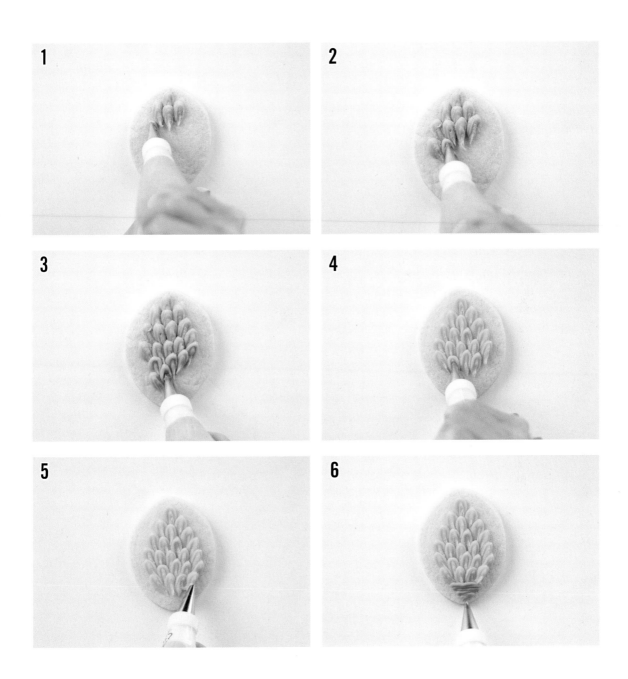

Sweet Pea Instructions

1. Use tip 104 and purple buttercream. Start in the top left corner and have your wide end facing toward you with the skinny end away from you. Pipe two small flowers with your bag at a 45-degree angle.

2. Pipe two other petals just under and add a third staggered down.

3. In the lower right of the cookie, pipe two small petals, one under the other.

4. Take green buttercream and tip 2 and pipe the base of the stem horizontally and come to a point.

5. Pipe stems to connect flowers and make curly vines.

6. Make tight curls just off the stems to bring the flower together.

MASTER TIP

If you tilt the piping bag closer to you on the sweet pea petals, it will form a small lip on the tops of the petals. Practice on a paper towel. For the lilacs, the petals will become larger the longer you allow the buttercream to billow out.

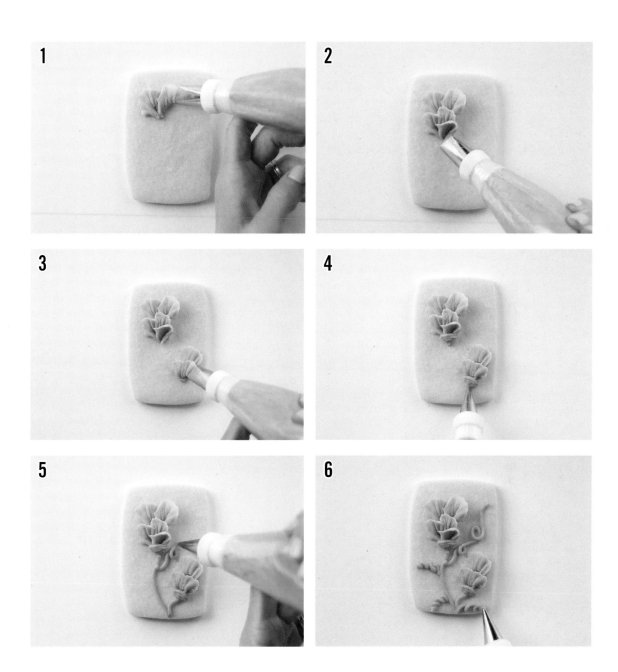

TEA TIME FLOWERS

The daffodil is bright and distinguished looking true to form. We have daffodil fields in the PNW filled with the most beautiful colors. Let your imagination run wild when you are choosing your colors for your cookie set. Yellow is traditional but with all the different species of daffodils, you can create some fun variations.

From the Kitchen	From the Drawer
Round cookies	Clean paintbrush
Batch of buttercream	Tips 104 and 2
	Yellow and purple gel food coloring

Pansy Instructions

1. Use dark purple buttercream and tip 104. Hold tip at a 45-degree angle and, in the top left part of cookie, pipe one petal. Hold the skinny end of the tip away from you.

2. Then pipe another petal with the same amount of pressure going up and then down.

3. Make a light purple layer with tip 104. Pipe on top but slightly under first petals so you can see the dark color below.

4. Turn the cookie upside down. Again, with the light purple, pipe in small up and down scalloped petals with the tip at a 45-degree angle.

5. Allow time for buttercream to crust over. Paint purple food coloring gel to paint the beard.

6. Lastly, use yellow buttercream and tip 2 to pipe a small circle in the middle for the pistil.

Daffodil on page 170

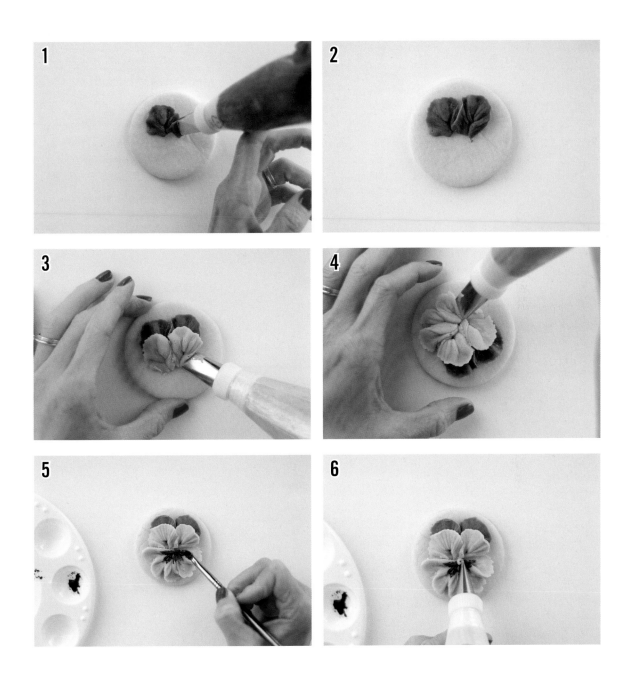

Daffodil Instructions

1. Start with yellow buttercream and tip 104. Hold the piping bag at a 45-degree angle with the skinny end facing away from you. Start in the center, apply pressure, and pipe up to create a skinny petal. Quickly come down.

2. Guide your piping bag with your other hand to steady yourself.

3. Keep piping around and make sure all six petals fit.

4. The sixth petal will close the flower.

5. Now, go to the center and hold the tip straight up and down so the skinny end is facing north. Create the trumpet by piping and turning your cookie.

6. Make the pistil in the center with tip 2. Pipe and slowly pull up, creating each tip.

MASTER TIPS

Pansies will be beautiful in any color; use two-toned buttercream on page 4 to add some white or yellow to the petals. Change the trumpet of the daffodil to an orange, darker yellow, or make the petals white and the trumpet peach. I zoomed out on a few Daffodil photos so you can see how my hand is holding the piping bag and directing at the same time.

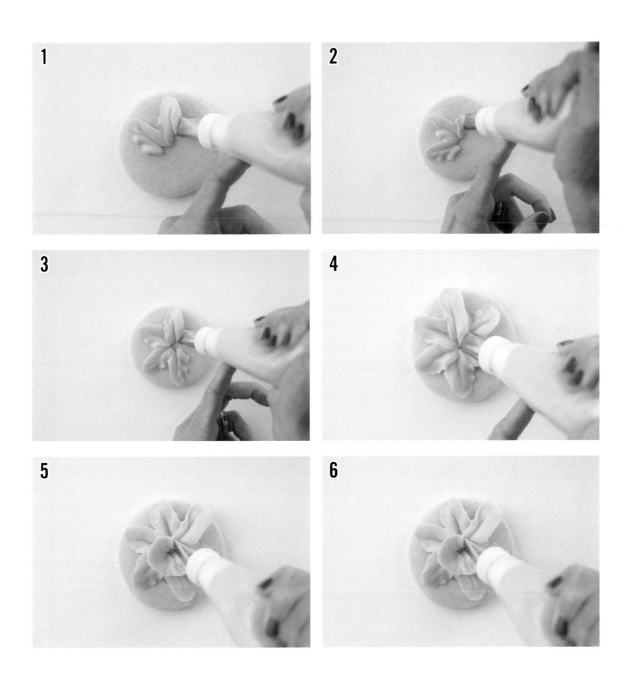

Sunny Day Flowers

page 174

Love Magnolias

page 180

SUNNY DAY FLOWERS

I can't help but smile looking at these cookies. These flowers are so happy and brighten up the darkest day. Sunflowers are a classic flower that I paired with the daisy because the petal technique is the same. This technique is one of the first flowers I ever created and it's become very popular as people put their own spin on this flower. If you keep building the petals up on the daisy, you will get a completely different flower.

I wanted to tie in a summer favorite, so I chose a dahlia. There are so many species of dahlias, and I have made so many variations of this flower. I chose this one because of its texture and its realistic look.

From the Kitchen	From the Drawer
Round cookies	Tips 104, 2, 18, 81, and 352
Batch of buttercream	White, yellow, brown, pink, fuchsia, and green gel food coloring

Daisy Instructions

1. Start with white buttercream and tip 104. Hold so the wide end of the tip is facing away from you. Start piping a tiny bit off the edge. Tip will be almost touching the cookie. Squeeze until the buttercream billows out sides and slowly pull back for each petal.

2. Pipe around to create a second layer slightly under the first.

3. Close the center.

4. Use tip 2 and yellow buttercream to make the center circle.

5. Make tiny dots on top.

6. Completed daisy.

Sunflower on page 176
Gerbera on page 177
Dahlia on page 178

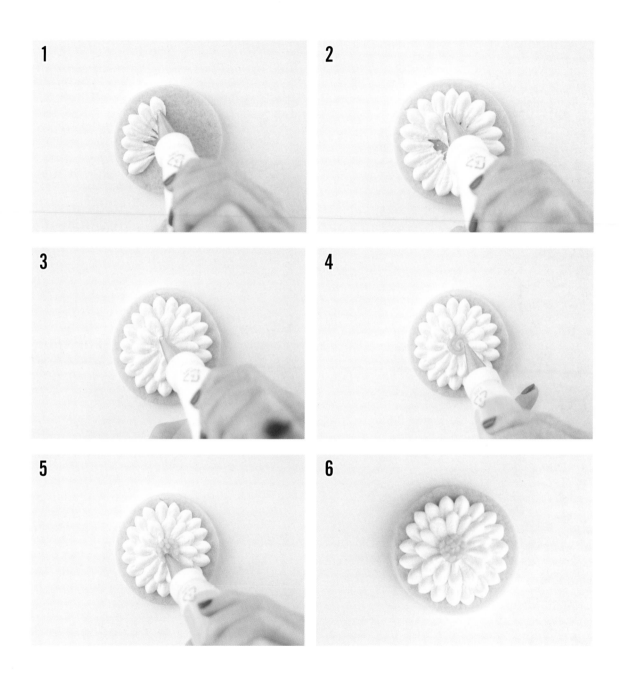

Sunflower Instructions

1. Use yellow buttercream and tip 104. Hold so the wide end of the tip is facing away from you. Start piping a tiny bit from the edge. Tip will be almost touching the cookie. Squeeze until the buttercream billows out sides and slowly pull back for each petal.

2. Pipe a second layer just slightly under the first.

3. Keep piping all the way around but leave a center that you will fill in with brown.

4. With brown buttercream and tip 18, pipe the center of sunflower. Hold tip straight up and down.

5. Pipe until the center is full.

6. Completed sunflower.

Gerbera daisy Instructions

1. Start with tip 104 and pink buttercream. Face the skinny end away from you. Pipe a little off the edge so the petals don't get smashed. In short motions, go up and down with the same amount of pressure.

2. Keep turning your cookie as you go to create an even flow of petals.

3. This back and forth motion will not need any wrist movement. Keep piping until the first layer is completed.

4. Pipe a second layer just under the first.

5. Attach tip 2 and pipe a round center.

6. Add tiny dots on top.

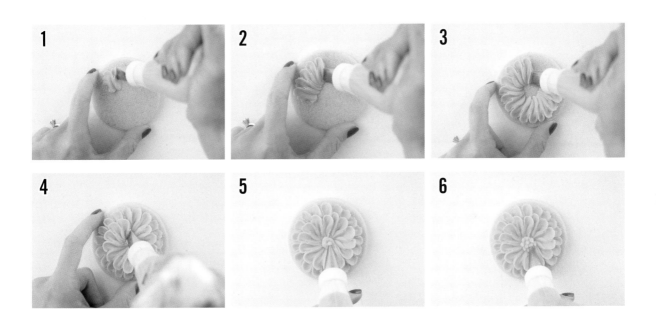

Dahlia instructions

1. Take your fuchsia buttercream and tip 104. The skinny end will be facing away from you and the wide end towards you. Hold the bag at a 45-degree angle and start piping the petals in short and small piping motions, going up and down.

2. Keep piping around the outside of your cookie but not the very edge.

3. Make a second layer of petals but leave some room to make one last layer of petals.

4. The third layer of petals will be small and tight.

5. For the center, use pink and tip 81. Pipe from the center and pull outward and upward to stagger and bunch the petals. Where you stop squeezing, the petal will end.

6. Take white buttercream and tip 2 and pipe the pistil of the flower. Start piping and gently pull up and then stop squeezing to break the buttercream.

MASTER TIPS

When piping the sunflower and daisy cookies, the longer you allow your buttercream to billow out before pulling down on each petal, the wider the petal will be. Practice on a paper towel. For piping the dahlia and gerbera daisy, the motion will not be in the wrist, but in the up and down movements for each petal. If you angle the piping bag towards you, you will get a tiny lip on the petals that will fold in.

LOVE MAGNOLIAS

So many songs about magnolias come to mind when I see this plate of cookies. Thomas Rhett's song "Marry Me" always plays in my head. Are you singing it, too?

White magnolias have Southern charm that is undeniable and hard not to simply adore. Use that inspiration as you make these flowers and they will turn out more beautiful than you imagine. (Use leaf-shaped cookies and just pipe the magnolia leaf on to add to your cookies set.)

From the Kitchen	From the Drawer
Square cookies	Tips 125, 123, 363, 104, and 2
Batch of buttercream	Green and white food coloring

Instructions

1. Start with green buttercream and tip 125. No need for a coupler for this one. Hold with the wide side of the tip facing in and the skinny end facing away from you. At a 45-degree angle, start piping up with the same amount of pressure, slow down at the top, and slowly pipe back to create first leaf.

2. Guide your hand with your other hand, as pictured. Pipe up and down. In another corner of the cookie, pipe third leaf.

3. Use petal tip 123 with the white buttercream. With the skinny side of the tip facing away from you at a 45-degree angle, pipe first petal up, around, and down.

4. Pipe a second petal. The base will have three, so spread accordingly.

5. For the second layer of petals, make them smaller and pipe them offset so each goes in between. There will be three of these petals.

6. Use 104 and white buttercream to pipe the third and smallest of the three petals.

7. Use light green buttercream and tip 363 to pipe the stamen.

8. Use tip 2 and pipe tiny carpels that look like dots.

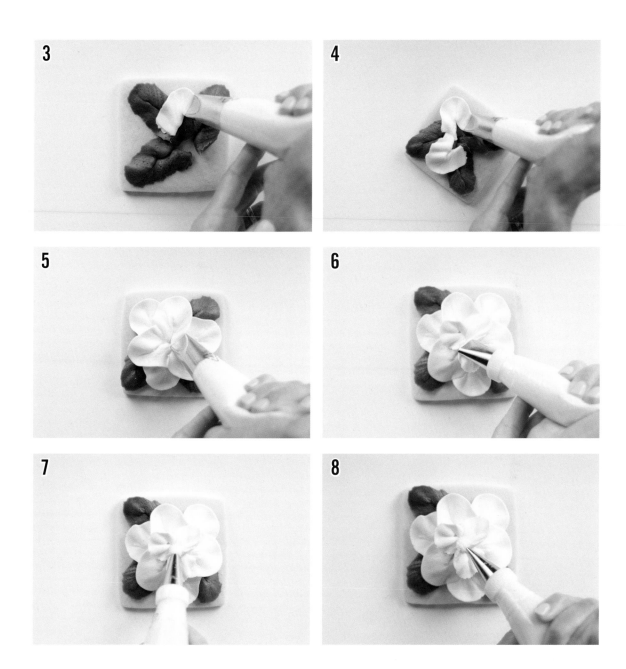

Flowers Bloom

page 184

Summer Love Flowers

page 188

FLOWERS BLOOM

This cookie plate of beautiful buttercream blooms gives me all the spring feels. I love the multicolored center of each flower. These flowers were inspired by some of the flower dresses I love to wear with bright and happy colors.

I like to switch up the petals and the center with lighter and darker shades of different colors. They can match any theme. I made a set of these flowers on rectangle-shaped cookies.

For the white flower, you will need yellow and pale yellow to make the center; it looks really beautiful and realistic this way.

From the Kitchen	From the Drawer
Round cookies	Tips 104, 21, and 2
Batch of buttercream	White, green, yellow, pink, and fuchsia gel food coloring

Pink Flower Instructions

1. Using pale green buttercream and tip 104, hold the piping bag with the wide part of the tip facing down and toward you and the skinny end up and away from you.

2. Pipe three leaves as your base. Pipe up, around, and down for each leaf.

3. Then, with pink buttercream and tip 104, start piping your first petal and make tiny motions to bunch the buttercream together to get the textured look of the petal.

4. Make five petals for the first layer.

5. Make smaller petals and stagger them for the second layer. Quit squeezing as you pull in to give it a smooth break on the fifth petal.

6. Use tip 2 and white buttercream and make a circle in the center with tiny dots.

7. Take tip 2 and fuchsia and pipe small dots of buttercream to fill in the center.

8. Make a circle around the white as well and that will finish off the flower.

White Flower page 186

White Flower Instructions

1. Use white buttercream and tip 104. Have your wide end facing towards you and the skinny end facing away from you and angle your bag at a 45-degree angle. Pipe and round each petal.

2. Don't pipe to the very edge but continue around your cookies, creating small round petals.

3. Give yourself room for five petals on the first layer.

4. Make a second but smaller layer and stagger the petals on top of each other. There will be five petals on the second layer.

5. Take tip 21 and pale yellow and pipe a dollop of buttercream in the middle, slowly pull up and stop squeezing, and then pull up to make the pistil of the flower. With darker yellow and tip 2, pipe lines in each crease of the light yellow to meet at the center. Then from the base of the center pipe outward to draw on the stamen.

6. Make little dots sporadically to create a realistic look to complete flower.

MASTER TIP

Rounding your wrist will make the petals round. You can leave the leaf out at the beginning of the pink flower and add in leaves with tip 352 at the end.

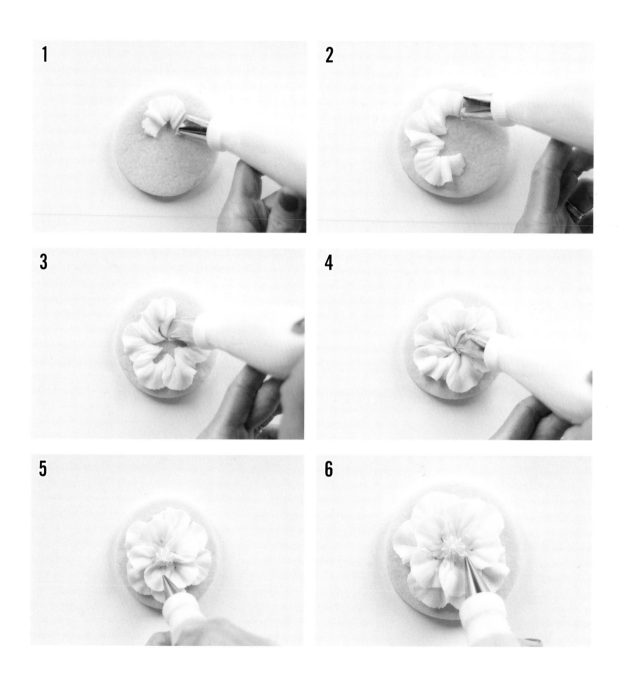

SUMMER LOVE FLOWERS

"Poppies. Poppies will put them to sleep," is an iconic line from The Wizard of Oz. *These poppies won't put you to sleep. Can you imagine them in orange, white, or pink too? Poppies are one of my favorite flowers, and last summer we found one growing almost as big as my face.*

I decided to share this particular Chrysanthemum flower because it's less difficult (but no one will ever guess it). It adds a pretty late summer feel to your cookie plate.

I added in a cotton flower because they are so simple and yet so beautiful. They add life and a little summer feel.

From the Kitchen	From the Drawer
Round cookie	Tips 123, 2A, 103, 363, and 143
Batch of buttercream	White, red, green, black, pink, and brown gel food coloring

Poppy Instructions

1. Hold piping tip at a 45-degree angle with the skinny end facing away from you. With bright red buttercream and tip 123, start in the center of cookie and pipe first petal, rounding your wrist.

2. Squeeze with a steady amount of pressure to create petals.

3. The bottom layer will have four petals.

4. For the top layer, make the petals smaller and add three.

5. Use dark green buttercream and tip 363. Pipe the pistil by holding piping bag straight up, squeeze, and pull up to lengthen. Stop squeezing to break the buttercream.

6. Use black buttercream and tip 2 and add tiny dots around the pistil and on the tip.

Chrysanthemum page 190
Cotton page 190

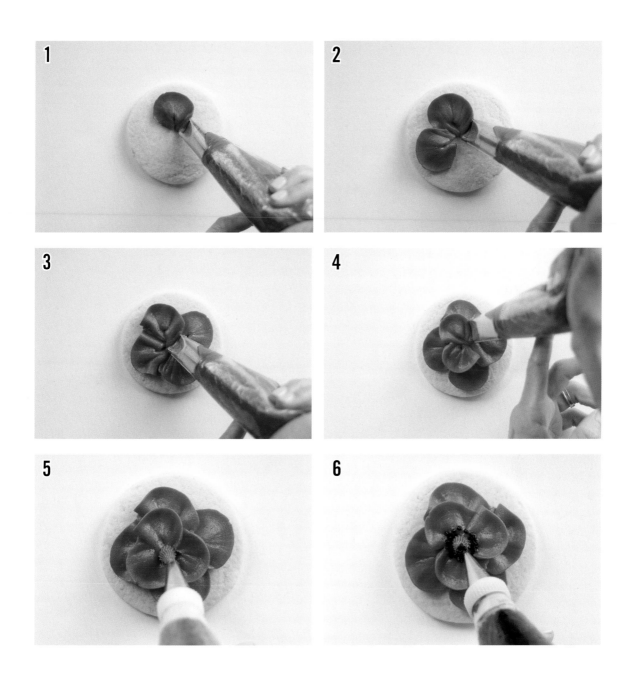

Chrysanthemum Instructions

1. Use tip 143 and pink buttercream. Hold the tip at an angle with the end up. Start in the middle of cookie, apply pressure, and pull back at the same time to make one long petal. Keep piping petals and turn your cookie as you go.

2. Pipe around the cookie leaving some space in the center; start to stagger the petals on the second layer so you can see the ones underneath.

3. As you pipe the center, pull the petals upward to close the center.

Cotton Instructions

1. Pipe center with brown buttercream and tip 103. In the center, make a star by having the skinny end face away from you. Pipe straight up and down, almost touching the cookie. Squeeze a little amount and stop.

2. With white buttercream and tip 2A, pipe big cotton dollops between the star tips. Pipe five all the way around.

3. Again, with the brown buttercream, pipe the tips in between each white mount. The tip will be facing away from you.

MASTER TIP

Change the poppy color to anything vibrant. Pipe petals on a paper towel first to get familiar with the rounding of the poppy. Change up the buttercream on the Chrysanthemum for a fall-themed cookie plate. Try tip 81 to get a smaller Chrysanthemum using this same technique.

Celebrations

Celebrate birthdays, a wedding, anniversary, welcoming a baby, the end of a fun sports season, or just celebrate the fact that you are a dog lover.

There's always time to celebrate something, and I've got the perfect cookies to help you do that!

Baby Reveal

page 202

WEDDING DREAMS

Most of us dream of a big, beautiful wedding that blows everyone away. While I think every-one has a different idea of a dream wedding, mine was super small in our church. So simple and perfect. My sister's wedding was big, beautiful, and planned to the very last detail. No matter your dream wedding, these cookies will make any bride gleam with joy. Use them as wedding favors or as Save the Date gifts.

From the Kitchen
Cake-, ring-, flower-, and leaf-shaped cookies
Batch of buttercream

From the Drawer
Absolut vodka or lemon extract
New paintbrush
Egyptian Gold Luster Dust
White and pink sugar pearls or nonpareils
Tips 104, 18, 4, 103, 2, and 5
Pink, fuchsia, green, black, and white gel food coloring

Cake Instructions

1. Mix a couple drops of vodka in the luster dust. I mix it in the lid of the container. Paint the cake stand on the cake.

2. Pipe with tip 4 and white buttercream back and forth horizontally to cover the top tier.

3. Attach tip 104 and pipe ruffles on the bottom tier. Pipe with the skinny end of the tip out and the wide side touching the cookie.

4. Attach tip 18 and make three rosettes in the center. To pipe a rosette, hold straight up and down a little off the base. Apply pressure and pipe down and then around in a circle and back down to connect. Decrease pressure as you connect, stop pressure, and pull away.

Ring on page 198
Leaf on page 200
Wedding Flower on page 200

Ring Instructions

1. Mix a couple drops of vodka in the luster dust in the lid of the container. Paint the metal of the ring.

2. With tip 4 and white buttercream, outline and fill ring. Pipe over the lines of the diamond.

3. Use pink buttercream and tip 103 to make a small peony. Pipe small strips that overlap with the wide end of the tip facing in and the skinny end facing away from you. Hold at an angle.

4. Make the petals longer as you go around.

5. Use dark green and tip 2 to pipe ferns. Squeeze buttercream and pull down for the top one. Pull to the side into the middle, alternating on each side until the desired size.

6. With tip 18, pipe a small light pink rosette.

7. Use fuchsia buttercream and pipe a small cluster with tip 2.

8. Use tip 2 and black buttercream to pipe on writing or date.

Leaf Instructions

1. Attach tip 5 to light green and outline leaf.
2. Fill in by piping horizontally back and forth. Hold the bag at an angle toward you so it flows out like a tube of toothpaste.
3. Draw the leaf vein down the center.

MASTER TIP

Change the colors to match any color palette. Design the cake to match the couples' wedding cake. You can also use tip 4 on the leaf instead of tip 5.

Wedding Flower Instructions

1. Start with light green buttercream and tip 104. Make two leaves. Hold with skinny side of tip facing away from you and fat end almost touching the cookie. Hold at a 45-degree angle and pipe up and back down for both leaves.
2. Pipe the first petal with tip 104. Hold with skinny end of tip facing away from you at a 45-degree angle. Begin to pipe around the first arch in a slight rounding motion.
3. Keep piping to add more petals.
4. Turn your cookie as you go and fill in flower.
5. The petals inside will get small and tight.
6. Add sugar pearls to center.

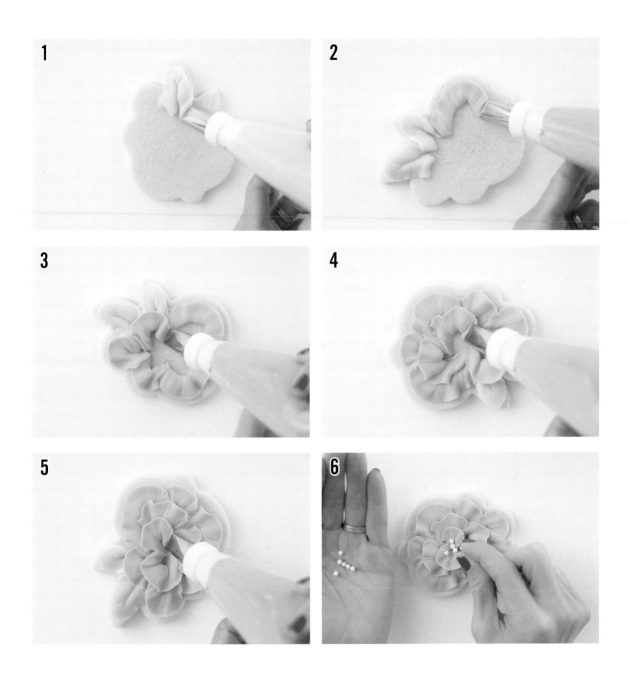

BABY REVEAL

So fun to break open a cookie to see what the gender of your baby will be. I had the honor of attending an appointment, was given the envelope, and was the only one who knew the sex of the baby until the mom- and dad-to-be cut open the cake. So much anticipation for the day and the reveal. For this cookie set, I wanted to bring that same idea of cutting into a cake to breaking open a cookie. It's such a fun and exciting moment to be a part of. When revealing the baby's gender, what if everyone at the party took a bite of their special cookie at the same time! Then you could really include people you love.

From the Kitchen	From the Drawer
Duck-, heart-, and onesie-shaped cookies	Angled spatula
Batch of buttercream	Tips 10, 12, 2, 5, and 103
Cup of hot water	Yellow, pink, blue, and white gel food coloring

Gender Reveal Heart Instructions

1. With tip 10 and pink or blue buttercream, pipe holding bag straight up and down. Hold close to cookie. You want the buttercream to come out flat. Pipe a small heart in the center.

2. Then with white buttercream and tip 12, pipe around the blue and cover up the blue.

3. Use my smooth buttercream technique on page 3.

4. Pipe a small border around the heart, using tip 2 and yellow buttercream.

5. Write *baby* on the heart.

6. Break open for surprise.

MASTER TIPS

Add a ruffle to the onesie for a girl or a bowtie for a boy. I love the *"waddle baby be"* theme, but you could do anything with these cookies and they would be darling.

Baby Duck on page 204
Onesie on page 205

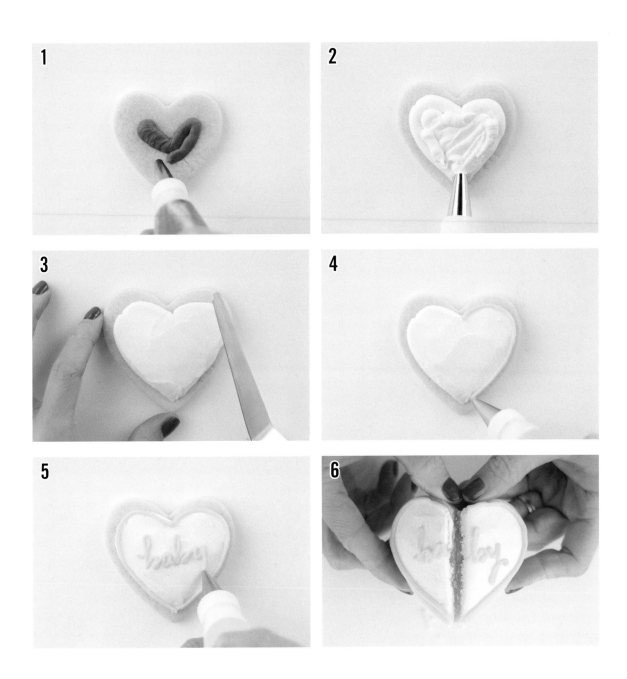

Baby Duck Instructions

1. Outline the duck with yellow and tip 5.

2. Fill in duck by piping horizontally back and forth while holding your bag at an angle so it comes out like a tube of toothpaste.

3. Use my smooth buttercream technique on page 3.

4. Outline duck with tip 5.

5. Attach tip 103, pipe ruffles on the duck. Hold piping bag at an angle with wide side of tip facing you and skinny side facing away from you. Make two layers of the ruffled feathers.

6. Completed duck.

Onesie Instructions

1. Outline and fill in onesie with tip 10. Hold piping bag straight up and down close to cookie and pipe flat.
2. Use my smooth buttercream technique on page 3.
3. Outline onesie with yellow buttercream and tip 2. Pipe at an angle so the buttercream flows like a tube of toothpaste.
4. Make lines from the legs, and across for the buttons on the bottom.
5. Make two lines on the sleeves.
6. Pipe a little duck on the chest.

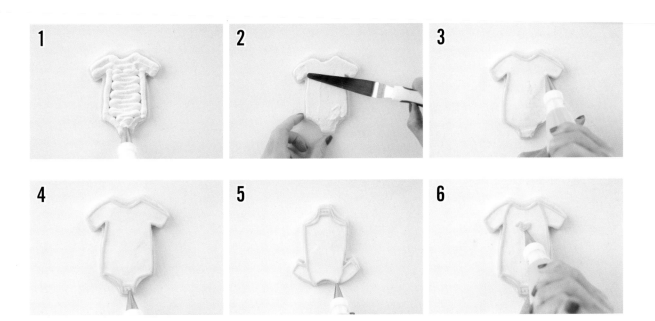

Celebrate the Day

page 208

Puppy Love

page 212

CELEBRATE THE DAY

I decided to use a cute letter board so that you can design it with any fun inspirational quote, bible verse, movie line, or song. My family absolutely loved these cookies so much. They were fun to design. Enjoy making them your own!

From the Kitchen
Large square-, balloon-, and cupcake-
   shaped cookies
Batch of buttercream

From the Drawer
Birthday sprinkles
Tips 2, 5, 10, 21, and 47
Pink, black, yellow, and white gel food
   coloring.

Letter Board Instructions

1. Start with light pink buttercream and tip 10. Hold the tip angled so it pipes out like a tube of toothpaste. Leave room on all four sides to pipe a border.

2. Pipe down the cookie.

3. Use white buttercream and tip 47 with the smooth side facing up. Pipe a border along the bottom.

4. Pipe border around the sides, hiding any uneven lines from the pink.

5. Use black buttercream with tip 2 to pipe writing.

6. Completed letter board.

Cupcakes on page 210
Balloon on page 210

Balloon Instruction

1. Outline and fill the balloon with tip 5.
2. Use my smooth buttercream technique on page 3.
3. With white buttercream, add a small line in top corner.

MASTER TIPS

Change the colors of the letter board to gray or white. Colors can fit any theme. Add sugar crystals to balloon.

1  **2**  **3**

Cupcake Instructions

1. Use yellow buttercream and tip 2 to pipe the candle fire.
2. Use tip 5 and pink buttercream to pipe two lines straight down for the candle.
3. Turn cookie to side, attach tip 10 to light pink buttercream. Pipe in a steady stream back and forth until the cupcake liner is filled.
4. Use white buttercream with tip 21 and pipe on frosting. Make wavy motions.
5. Add birthday sprinkles.
6. Completed cupcake.

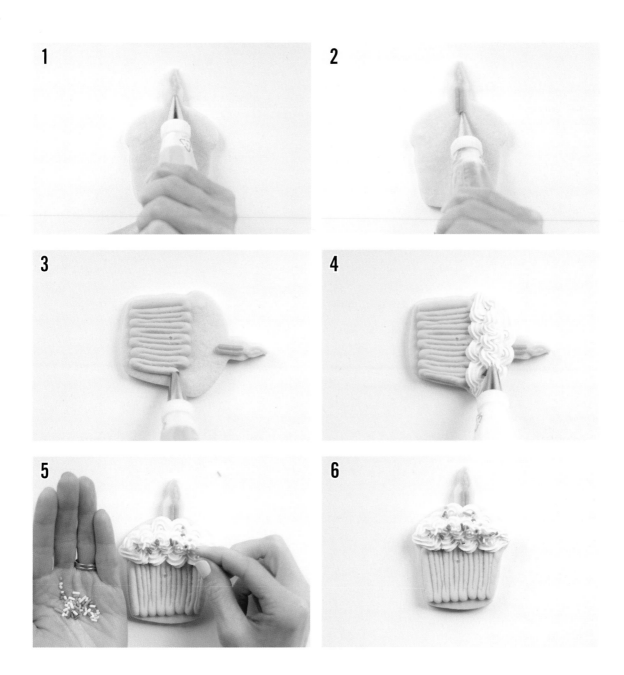

PUPPY LOVE

These dog cookies are so fun. I came up with them for a TV segment and they stuck. After my segment, my son Mikie watched my tutorial, grabbed a piping bag, and re-created the cookie perfectly. It's all in the details.

I can make any dog into an easy, delicious buttercream-frosted cookie. I'm very careful on where I place the eyes and nose specific to each dog. Then I take marshmallows, color them, and cut them in half for the little tongues (see page 220). They seriously can't get any cuter!! The best part is that they are done on simple, round cookies.

From the Kitchen
Round cookies
Batch of buttercream

From the Drawer
Black sugar pearls
Mini semisweet chocolate chips
Regular semisweet chocolate chips
Mini marshmallows
New paintbrush
Tweezers
Tips 12 and 18
Brown, white, and black gel food coloring

Cavalier King Charles Spaniel Instructions

1. Use white buttercream and star tip and pipe the white coloring of the face. Hold piping bag straight up and down, squeeze, and release to pipe the star. Keep going to outline desired shape.

2. On the bottom where the nose will be, pipe a second layer of buttercream to make it stand off the cookie higher.

3. Use light brown buttercream and tip 18. Pipe the eyes and long ears.

4. Pipe a second layer over the ears to make them stand off the cookie. Place two mini chocolate chips for the eyes, but be careful on placement. Use tweezers.

5. Turn a mini chocolate chip to the side to place the nose.

6. Place tongue on mouth.

MASTER TIPS

The second layer of buttercream on the nose and ears are crucial for making this cookie look like the pup. Placing the mini chocolate chips closer together for the eyes, gives the Cavalier King Charles Spaniel an accurate representation. Make the pup all white to change the dog entirely.

Poodle on page 214
Lab on page 216
French Bull Dog on page 218
Norwich Terrier on page 220

Poodle Instructions

1. Pipe the top part of cookie with star tip 18 with black and white buttercream (our poodle is an old man). Apply pressure while holding piping bag straight up and down. Squeeze, release and pull up for each star.

2. Fill in the top part.

3. Use white buttercream and tip 18 to make the nose. Make into a pointed shape and fill in.

4. Pipe ears by overlapping part of the head you already piped in black and white. Pipe down the sides and pipe on a second layer of buttercream just on the ears so they stand out on the cookie. Also make three dollops where the eyes would be.

5. On the larger white part of the face, place mini chocolate chip with point down for the nose. Then, carefully place two black sugar pearls for the eyes.

6. Place tongue just under the little nose.

MASTER TIPS

I used the two-toned buttercream (see page 4) for the black because my sister's poodle Charlie has gray hair. Make this pup all black or brown and change to a golden doodle. If you use brown, change the nonpareils to mini chocolate chips with the tip straight down in the buttercream.

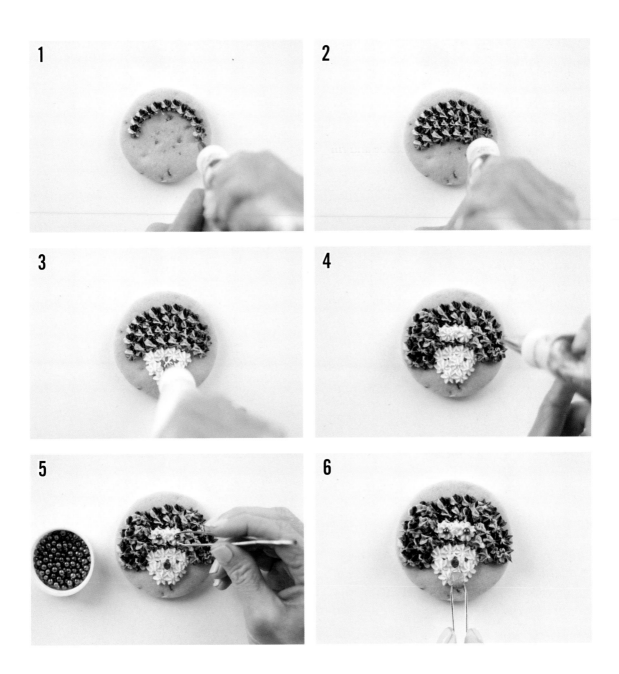

Lab Instructions

1. Use light brown buttercream with tip 12 attached. Hold piping bag straight up and down just slightly off the cookie, squeeze bag until buttercream billows out sides, and stop. This will make the dots for the pup. Pipe five along the very top.

2. Pipe four directly under, and then three. Pipe two and one to pipe in an upside-down triangle.

3. On the center dot on the third row, create a larger dollop of buttercream so it stands off the cookie for the nose.

4. Pipe each ear from the fifth row down to the third row.

5. With tweezers, place the mini chocolate chips for the eyes tip-down; placement is important.

6. For the nose, use a chocolate chip with the tip down in the center of the big dollop you made earlier.

7. Place the tongue just under the nose.

8. Completed pup.

MASTER TIPS

This pup is so simple and can be used for many breeds. I originally made this to look like a golden retriever. Use black buttercream or dark brown for black and chocolate labs. Make it white and pipe small black spots for a Dalmatian. There are so many possibilities, just remember that the placement of the eyes and nose are important.

1

2

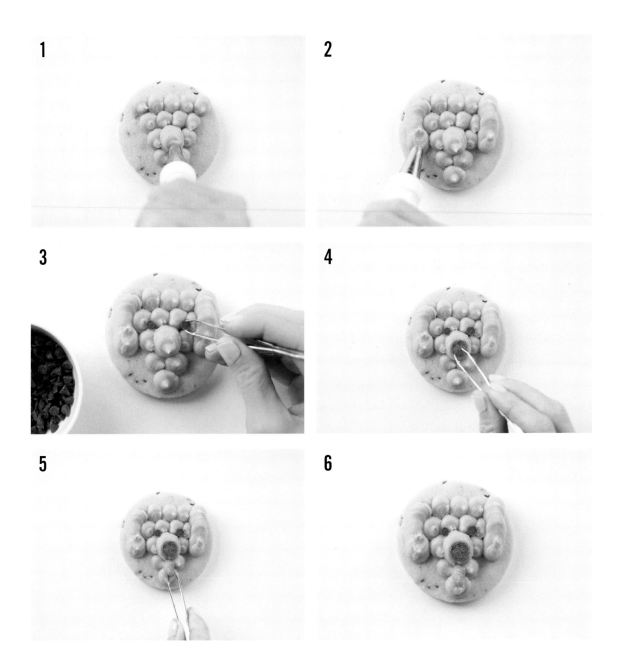

French Bulldog Instructions

1. Use tip 12 with black buttercream. Pipe straight up and down just off the cookie. Start at the top and pipe two ears. Start squeezing and go up, round the top slightly, and come down.

2. Pipe around the bottom to frame the face. Make it an oval turned on its side. Fill in the face by making dollops, stop and pull up to break the buttercream off.

3. Make the Frenchie mouth stand up by piping from the bottom up to the middle of the face and back down to the other side. It will stand higher than the rest of the cookie.

4. Place the eyes carefully; they will be spread apart.

5. Turn a chocolate chip upside down and place it in the middle of the mouth you piped sticking off the cookie.

6. Place tongue just under the nose.

MASTER TIPS

The mouth and snout of this pup needs to be precise. The placement of the eyes is very important because you want it to look accurate. You can make this cookie into a pug by simply making the ears small, keeping the buttercream all black or changing the face to a tan buttercream.

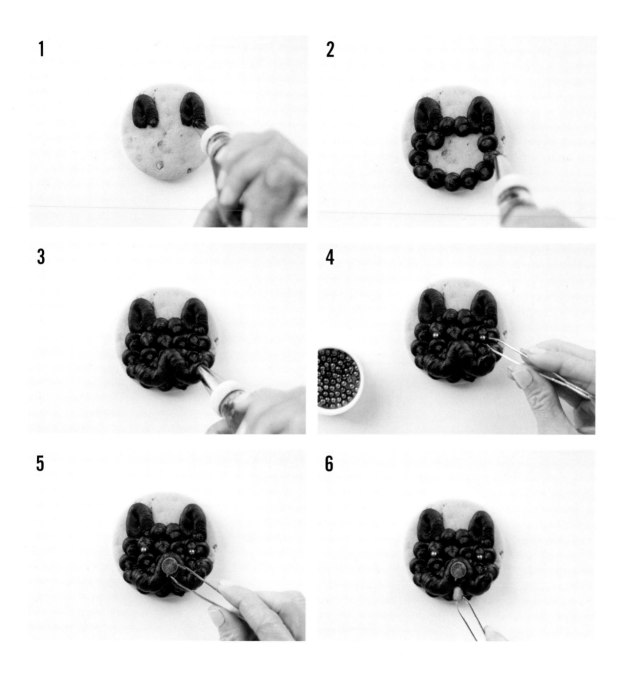

Norwich Terrier Instructions

1. Use brown and tip 18. Apply pressure while holding piping bag straight up and down. Squeeze, release, and pull up for each star. Pipe two triangles at the very top with five stars each.

2. Frame the face and make it long, not perfectly round. Fill it in.

3. Hold the piping bag at an angle and pipe two wisps of buttercream on the tips of both ears. Make two more for the eyebrows at the top of the face.

4. Pipe four longer strands of buttercream on the bottom of the face to make a beard. Just above that, pipe a mustache like you did with the eyebrows.

5. Carefully place two black sugar pearls for the eyes just under the eyebrows. Place a mini chocolate chip with the point down, right in the middle of the mustache.

6. Place the tongue just under the mustache, on the beard.

MASTER TIPS

This cookie is so versatile as it can be used to make many breeds of dogs by simply changing the buttercream colors to fit your pup. The wisps of hair on the ears, mouth, and chin can be removed as well. Change a few details to make it a Chihuahua by using a tip 10 instead of the star tip and spread eyes apart, build up nose a little like we did with the Lab, and add a regular-sized chocolate chip.

Pink Tongue Instructions

Lay down a piece of parchment paper. Cut mini marshmallows in half and place them sticky-side down. Mix pink food coloring with a little water and paint on the marshmallow. You can cut it into fourths if half is too big. Let dry for an hour before use. Store unused pieces in plastic bag.

I can do all things through Christ who strengthens me. **Philippians 4:13**

SPORTS

One of our favorite inspirational football movies is Facing the Giants. *If you haven't seen it, it's a must-watch. I love the part of the death crawl, when they're on the field and the coach wants their absolute best.*

We've all got giants to face in our lives; this plate of cookies is inspired by watching my kids play their hearts out and never give up.

From the Kitchen	**From the Drawer**
Football- and round-shaped cookies	Angled spatula
Batch of buttercream	Tips 2, 5, and 18
Cup of hot water	Brown, orange, red, black, and white gel food coloring

Football Instructions

1. Outline football with brown buttercream and fill in with tip 5.
2. Use my smooth buttercream technique on page 3.
3. Outline football again on the edge.
4. With white buttercream and tip 5, pipe a line at the top for the laces.
5. Then pipe the laces across the line, making four.
6. Finished football.

MASTER TIPS

The star tip will also work for the football. Use the volleyball technique to make a soccer ball.

Basketball on page 226
Volleyball on page 228
Baseball on page 229

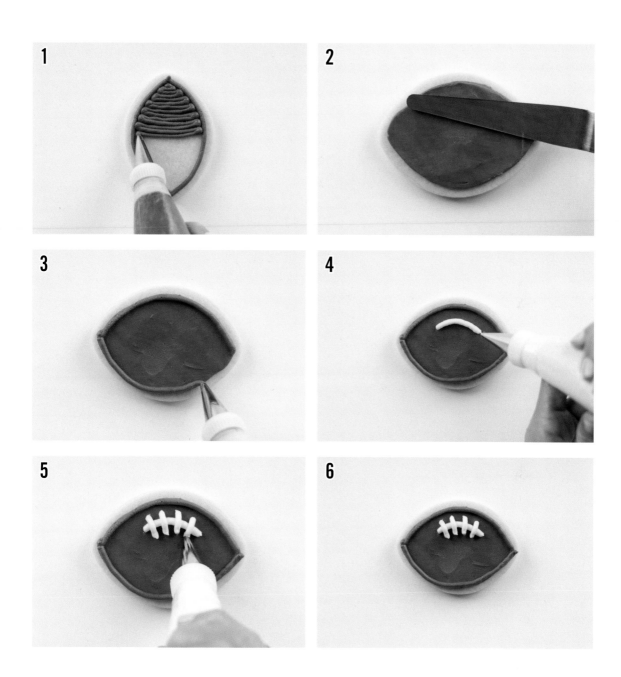

Basketball Instructions

1. Use tip 5 and brown buttercream. Pipe a half circle on the far left and right sides of the basketball. Pipe at an angle so it flows like a tube of toothpaste.

2. Pipe a vertical line down the center of the two half circles.

3. Then pipe a horizontal line across the center.

4. Use tip 18 with orange buttercream. Hold piping bag straight up and down just off the surface of the cookie. Start to squeeze buttercream until it puffs out the sides, stop squeezing and pull up.

5. Fill the entire cookie with orange.

6. Completed basketball.

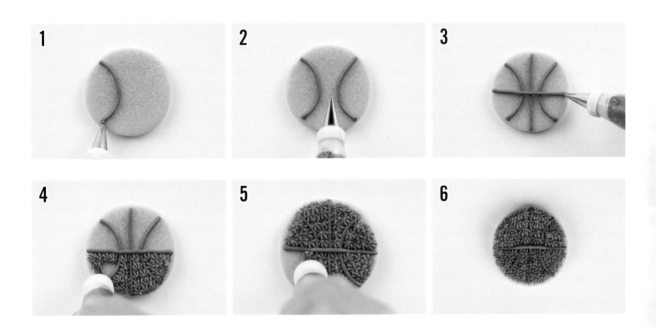

Volleyball Instructions

1. Use tip 2 with black buttercream and separate the volleyball into three.
2. In the upper right, draw three lines.
3. Turn cookie and repeat. Turn the cookie a final time and draw the last three lines.
4. Use white buttercream and tip 5 to fill in the sections. Pipe back and forth horizontally all the way down.
5. Fill each section and turn the cookie.
6. Repeat until each section is filled.

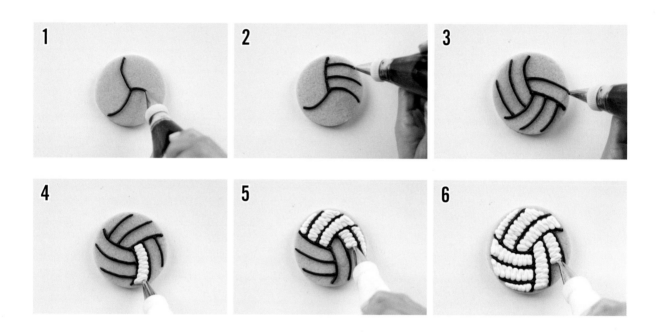

Baseball Instructions

1. Use white buttercream with tip 12 attached. Hold the bag straight up and down for flatter piping. Outline and fill from the outside, inward.
2. Use my smooth buttercream technique on page 3.
3. Use tip 2 and red buttercream to pipe the half-circle lines on the left and right side of the cookie.
4. Pipe little V laces.
5. Continue down the first side.
6. Turn cookie upside down and repeat the V's down the other side to complete the baseball.

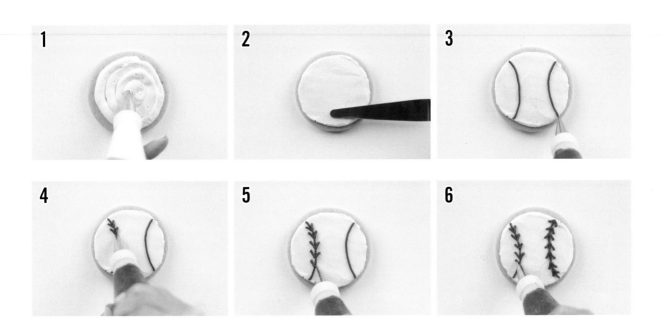

Bonus

The bonus chapter has some of the special cookies I wanted to feature on the cover but didn't quite make it into a cookie set. I worked very hard to have a cover that took you through more seasons than one. Here you will find some of my favorite designs I didn't want you to miss, plus everyone likes a bonus chapter!

FALL TREE

The Pacific Northwest is breathtaking in the fall. I wanted to capture some beauty in the changing leaves that we get to enjoy every year, so I turned our fall trees into a cookie. I'm always inspired by nature and I often try to turn what I see and appreciate into cookies, which makes for the best and most original ideas, I believe. I used a large leaf cookie cutter but you can also use a round tree or a flower bouquet cookie cutter and use this same idea. Use your imagination to make it your own. Make a fuller tree by adding more branches and leaves.

From the Kitchen	From the Drawer
Tree-shaped cookies Batch of buttercream frosting	Tips 352 and 5 Orange, light green, dark green, and yellow gel food coloring

Instructions

1. Start by making a tree with your brown and tip 5.
2. Attach tip 352 and start with any shade, beak pointed down. Let the buttercream billow out and slowly move away from the branch.
3. Switch to light green. Go from the top of the branch to underneath and pipe your leaves.
4. Add in yellow buttercream leaves sporadically.
5. Switch to orange buttercream to complete the tree.
6. Fall tree complete.

MASTER TIP

I like to see a good amount of buttercream billow out before I slowly move my bag away to create the leaf. You can make the leaves all green if they're not going in a fall set of cookies. Or add some red apples for a darling apple tree cookie.

COLOR-CHANGING LEAF

This special cookie shows the beauty in the changing leaves. This flower uses my two-toned technique on page 4. I used three colors—red, orange, and yellow—to make this cookie really stand out. This cookie is simple but bold enough to add beauty in any fall-themed cookie set. This same technique can be used as a camp fire for a camp-out theme in the summer. Keep the leaf in shades of green also.

From the Kitchen
Leaf-shaped cookies
Batch of buttercream

From the Drawer
Tips 104 and 2
Brown, red, yellow, and orange gel food coloring

Instructions

1. With your fall-colored buttercream and tip 104, hold the wide end facing away from you and the skinny end toward you. Apply pressure to your bag so the buttercream billows out and slowly pull down.
2. Pipe down the right side of the leaf first.
3. Then pipe down the left side to fill in the entire cookie.
4. Guide your bag to bring the bottom of the leaves to the center.
5. Take brown buttercream and tip 2 and pipe the spine of the leaf with veins attaching.
6. Make a few vines on each side to complete the leaf.

MASTER TIPS

The buttercream will billow out the sides of the tip and as you ease up on the pressure and move down the cookie, it will become skinnier. Guide the piping bag to follow the shape of the leaf. You can easily make so many designs by piping and dragging the buttercream.

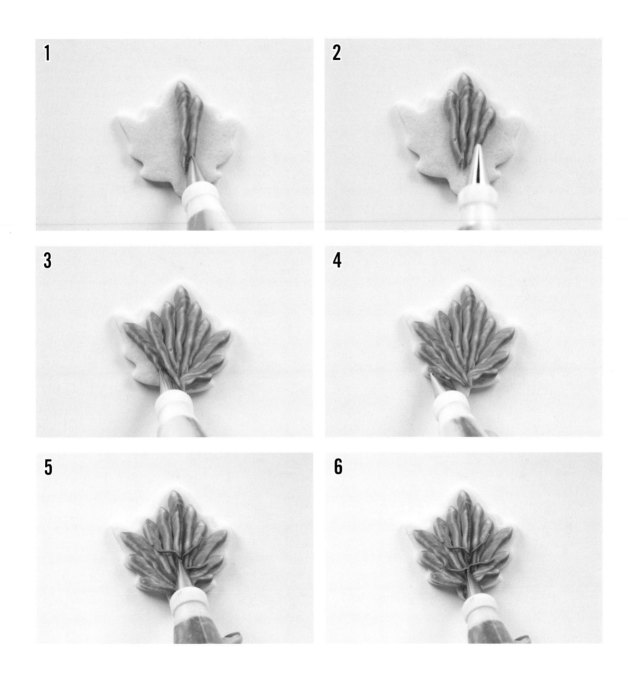

WHITE PUMPKIN

This sweet little pumpkin is on the cover of my book, and you can add it to so many different sets—even baby shower "little pumpkin" cookies. These pumpkins remind me of Cinderella-themed cookies, very whimsical. Don't they remind you of a fairy tale cookie? The vines are loosely laid on the pumpkin as if a magic wand was guiding them into place.

From the Kitchen
Pumpkin-shaped cookies
Batch of buttercream

From the Drawer
Tips 2, 5, and 10
White, brown, and green gel food coloring

Instructions

1. Outline your pumpkin with tip 5 and white buttercream.
2. Separate the cookie by drawing lines down the center so you can fill.
3. To fill the cookie, use tip 10 and squeeze buttercream out while slowly moving down to the bottom. This is my easy-fill method.
4. Continue until the cookie is filled.
5. Using brown and tip 2, make a stem with a back and forth motion.
6. To finish the pumpkin, use tip 2 and your green buttercream. Pipe tiny vines starting at the stem.

MASTER TIP

Make your pumpkins orange, yellow and orange, or light green to turn them into a Cinderella pumpkin. I've also made these in pink for baby shower themes.

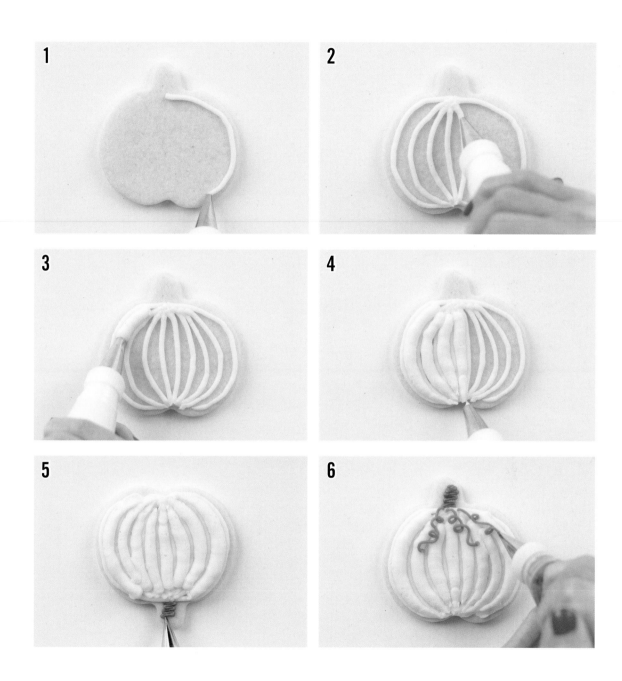

CACTUS

This cookie won't leave you stuck. Ha, there's another cookie pun for you. I love a fun desert theme with all kinds of cookies with different sizes of cacti. The amount of buttercream you get to use on this cookie is up to you. Make it higher and larger by simply making the center bigger vertically. You can have fun with this design and they will look so sharp when you are finished.

From the Kitchen	From the Drawer
Round cookies	Tips 363, 18, and 2
Batch of buttercream	Green and white gel food coloring

Instructions

1. Use tip 363 with green buttercream. Pipe a circle in the center but leave room on the edge.

2. Hold piping bag straight up and down and pipe on the edge on the cookie toward the center of the buttercream.

3. Continue to do this all the way around until you complete the cactus top.

4. Use white buttercream and tip 2 to pipe the spines on the cactus. Pipe four to five up each green section you piped.

5. Continue until the cactus is covered and looks prickly.

6. Attach tip 18 to the white buttercream. Hold piping bag straight up and down and pipe a star on the very top for the flower.

MASTER TIPS

Change the white flower to hot pink or yellow to show different colors of blooming cacti. The colors of flowers can change with the colors and the theme of your cookie set.

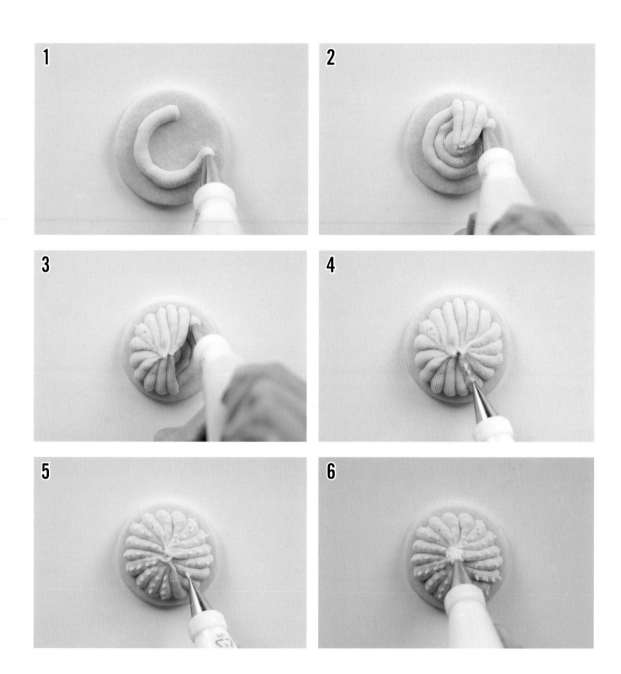

MISTLETOE TOP

This Mistletoe top is one of my original designs that I'm so proud of and I love seeing re-created. When I brainstorm ideas, I try to do things no one is doing yet. I was inspired by some Christmas movies on the Hallmark Channel that feature magic around kissing under the mistletoe. I thought it would be fun to have an aerial view of the beloved mistletoe that is simple enough for anyone to re-create. This cookie is beautiful and will add such a pretty touch to Christmas cookie plates.

From the Kitchen
Round cookies
Batch of buttercream

From the Drawer
White sugar pearls or nonpareils
Tip 104
Green and white gel food coloring

Instructions

1. Use dark green buttercream and tip 104. Hold piping tip at a 45-degree angle with the skinny end up and away from you and the wide end toward you and on the cookie. Start to squeeze and pipe the first leaf and slightly round your wrist in a quarter circle.

2. Pipe up, slightly round, and back down to the center.

3. Turn your cookie as you go and make five base petals.

4. For the middle, use light green buttercream with tip 104. Pipe four smaller petals on top.

5. Then back to dark green, pipe two very small leaves to complete the piping.

6. Add a cluster of white sugar pearls on top.

MASTER TIPS

Stagger the petals when you alternate colors so you can see the light green contrast with the dark green.

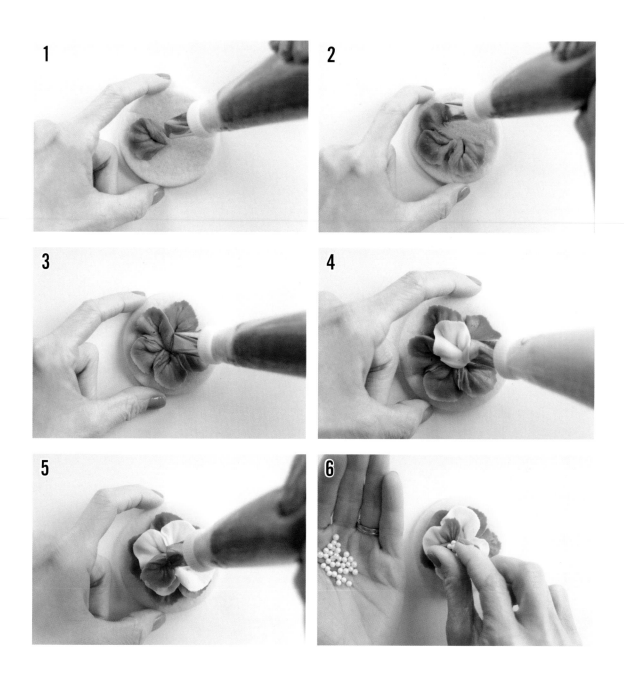

Acknowledgments

My husband, Mike

My best friend, my biggest supporter, and the man okay with being Mr. Hutch Oven. I thank you for encouraging me and pushing me to chase my dreams. This all wouldn't be possible without your constant love and support. Just look at all God has done for us; it's been hard at times, and losing Jenny broke us but didn't break us apart. It made us closer, and we found faith together. It's a miracle, and I'll fight together with you always. Years ago, I remember asking you if I was qualified to be doing this, and you grabbed me and stared me straight in the eyes and said, "Look at everything we have overcome and how far God has carried us. YOU are the MOST qualified." Thank you for never allowing me to settle and always saying "Babe, you've got this!" You and the kids are my world; we are forever, all in!

My daughter, Reese

My girl, my daughter, and my favorite woman in the entire world. Thank you for letting me be me and encouraging me to stay true to myself. There have been times when it would have been easy to let Satan win in certain situations, but you have always reminded me of who I am. Thank you for helping me believe in myself; I couldn't have done this without you. We have been through so much and I couldn't be prouder of who you are. I'm so lucky to be your mom. You are the first person I want to share good news with. You are always so happy for everyone and that is such a gift. Reesie, I love you more!

My son, Nick

Buddy, thank you for being excited every step of the way. I love having your support and I love every time you say, "Good job, Mom." I love how happy you are for me. I couldn't be where I am without you, bud. Every new cookie or new idea, I had to run by you to see what you thought. I value your opinion and can't thank you enough for standing behind me to help push this book together. You never give up on me and you inspire me to always keep working hard. Thank you for understanding how much work I was doing. I love you so much, Nick, thank you for keeping me strong.

My son, Mikie

Mikie, your support has meant so much to Mommy. I love how much pride you take in what I'm doing. It fills my heart that you love every video I've ever made and that you have watched them all so many times. Seeing you light up when amazing things happen for me is something very special. You listen to every crazy idea I have and tell me it's going to work. Thank you for being excited for me though it all. I love you more than you can imagine, and I couldn't have done this without you. You bring me light, Mikie, and remind me every day how much God loves us.

My angel daughter, Jenny

This book is for you, too, my Jenny. I miss you so much every single day. Your short life on Earth made me who I am today. I know you are in the arms of Jesus. I hear time in Heaven is different than time here on Earth. It brings me peace to believe that by the time you look around to see where I am, I'll be right up there with you. Thank you for making me the mom and person I was meant to be.

My mom, Jenny

Mom, thank you for being excited every single step of the way. Thank you for coming over when I've needed you. Thank you for holding down the fort when I've had to fly out of town. Your love and commitment to being a mother, no matter how old I get, inspires me to always be there for my children. You have taught me to stand up for myself, hold onto my values, and to fight for myself. This book has been grueling at times; your constant messages and phone calls to say "You can do it!" really kept me going. I love you more than words can say. Thank you for pushing me through to the finish line.

My sisters

I love you to the moon and back.

Jo

My sister, I remember sitting in your living room dreaming and planning the future. Your idea for me to write a book with step-by-step photos to help any baker decorate was brilliant. It really happened!!! Your support and encouragement through this have meant everything to me. Thank you for praying for me when you knew I needed it; you have been a light. Thank you for dropping everything to call me when I send group S.O.S texts. Thank you for really knowing how much this book means to me. I love you, sister.

Ali

Sister!!! We are really doing it, Hare! This has been a crazy whirlwind of emotions. Thank you for checking on me and for always offering to help. Just knowing you are there makes a big difference. Thank you for lightening my mood with funny GIFs when things are hard. You have always been a huge encouragement and

support for me, especially right now. Telling me "You can do it, Reg" helps me to believe I can and I will. Your unfailing love has helped bring me where I need to go. I love that when I call with things, you always ask me, "Well, is that what you want?" This helps me realize this is my life and I get to choose. I love you, Gert.

Patti

Sweet sister. I can't think of a better cheerleader in my life than you. I hear you say, "Good job, Mama!!!" and I smile. You have helped me so much through this book. I love how excited you always are when good things happen to me. Thank you being here for me and the kids. Your support means everything to me and having you cheer me on helped me push through. I think that if everyone had a Patti in their life, they would be so much happier. I love you forever, Pie.

Johannah

My talented photographer and dear friend. Who would have thought back in middle school that today we would be doing a book together? Isn't life crazy? Thank you for helping me through this and giving so much time to be at my house weekly for our shoots. I love our time through this and couldn't think of a better person to do it with. You are one of a kind and a true friend. Thank you and I love you, babe!

Alex and Christina

My dear friends, you both mean so much to me. Thank you for giving me encouragement, faithful prayers, and confidence. Thank you for helping me through this process. I value you both and I hope you know how much your friendship not only has helped me but helped my husband. This has been a lot for our family, both good and bad. There were times when I didn't think I could do it; you were there to remind me that God was paving the way. Thank you for always being so freaking happy for me, saying, "Lets always be this excited about this stuff!!!"

My bible study

Nicole, Stephanie, Julianna, Michelle, Heather, Andrea, Kala, Marisa, Sarah, and Sonya. Friends, I truly could not have done this without you all and your prayers. Your encouragement has helped me realize I can do anything. The texts and calls have meant so much through writing this book. You women are who I aspire to be more like. Your friendship means more to me than you can imagine. Thank you for loving me during this crazy time in my life. I love you all and treasure your friendships.

Heather, thank you for being such a big support for me through this book. Thank you for allowing us to use your barn. You would say its Cole's barn, but he says it's yours, so thank you both.

Andrea, I couldn't think of a better person I'd rather communicate via GIFs with. Haha, but seriously, you have helped me feel confident

with my book's purpose. You have encouraged me and reminded me that fear doesn't live here! You have helped my daughter and been a light. I am forever grateful for who you are in our life.

Julianna, you have talked me though a lot in this process, especially in the beginning. Thank you for praying for me and with me.

Nicole, you have been excited and supportive to me every step of the way. Thankful you always check in.

Megan

My friend, thank you for helping me get though life when things are hard. Thank you for celebrating things with me when they are exciting. Your prayers, checkup texts, and constant support has helped me so much. You have always encouraged me to share my story because it could help someone who is struggling. I will be forever grateful for your friendship, especially these past six months when my life was overwhelming.

Stephen

Dearest friend, I could write a novel on all the things! Thank you for being my person I can text anything to. The good, the bad, you know it all. Your sense of humor is just what I need. Thank you for believing in me, and in this book. Thank you for being my first baking buddy and for the fun times together. You know it's hard for me to make a decision sometimes, so thank you for helping me pick out the shoes when I can't. I love you forever!

Debbie

Thank you for believing in me. Everyone has that one person they refer back to when they need someone to believe in them. I'll never forget the first time we met, you gave me so much validation and encouragement when I shared my story with you. Thank you for your endorsement, for saying you believe in me, and saying, "Girl, this is all you! You are amazing!" Your words have brought me strength. I love you.

My church

The Grove Church in Marysville, Washington saved our lives. We are forever grateful to Nik and his incredible team. Thank you for praying for our family and encouraging us though this season of life.

My town

Arlington is where I was born and raised. Typically, acknowledgments aren't so broad, but I had to add in what a huge support everyone has been. My kids' teachers in the Arlington School District, their coaches, and the community has taken notice, encouraged, and been excited right along with me and my family. I can't thank you all enough.

My editor, Nicole Frail

I really can't thank you enough for ALL your hard work. You have helped me being my vision to life in this book. Thank you to the team at Skyhorse (Laura Klynstra, Daniel Brount, Mona Lin, Chris Schultz) for your hours upon hours of hard work.

About the Author

Emily Hutchinson is the founder of The Hutch Oven. She perfected her craft as a master decorator and loves teaching her original designs that make you fall in love with her style.

Emily started baking as a small child with her grandmother. As she grew into adulthood and became a mother, baking took a temporary back burner. Then in 2008, her daughter Jenny passed away from SIDS. She was beyond devastated. With no hope in sight, her friends invited her to church, and she started to bake again. Ten years later, her Instagram account has more than 100,000 followers, she has taught numerous classes, and appears on national television to showcase her popular techniques. She has found a beautiful way to honor her daughter Jenny and make her family proud.

Emily is a loving wife to her husband, Mike, and mother to Reese, Nick, and Mikie. Her first love is her family. When she isn't baking, Emily is attending bible study, volunteering at her children's school, and working out to stay healthy. Her children are a priority in her life and she loves supporting their dreams. Her girlfriends are very important to her. Her family attends church regularly, and they give back to the community when they can. Emily and her family love Jesus and thank God for His goodness and Grace over the years. Emily resides just outside of Seattle with her family.

Psalm 62: 1-2 *Truly my soul finds rest in God; my salvation comes from him. Truly he is my rock and my salvation; he is my fortress, I will never be shaken.*

Index

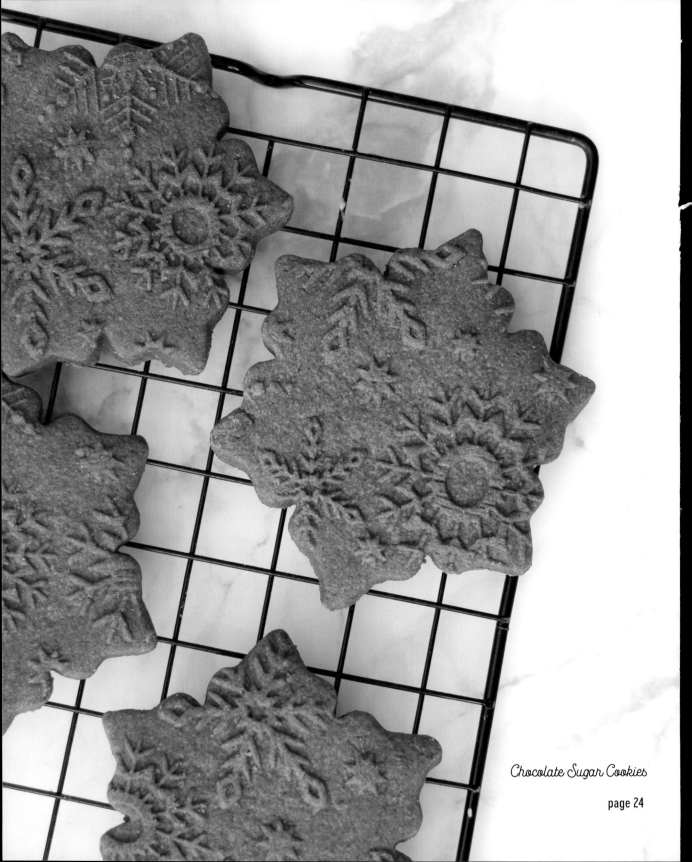

Chocolate Sugar Cookies

page 24